Madagascar Political Layout, a History.
A practice of Democracy.

Author
Noel Boba

SONITTEC PUBLISHING. All rights reserved. No part of this publication may be reproduced, distributed, or transmitted in any form or by any means, including photocopying, recording, or other electronic or mechanical methods, without the prior written permission of the publisher, except in the case of brief quotations embodied in critical reviews and certain other noncommercial uses permitted by copyright law. For permission requests, write to the publisher, addressed "Attention: Permissions Coordinator," at the address below.

Copyright © 2019 Sonittec Publishing
All Rights Reserved

First Printed: 2019.

Publisher:
SONITTEC LTD
College House, 2nd Floor
17 King Edwards Road,
Ruislip
London
HA4 7AE.

Content

Content 4

Madagascar Political Layout. 1
  Madagascar Political Insider Overview 1
  Madagascar Political Transformation 5
    Executive Summary 5
    History and Characteristics of Transformation 8
    Transformation Status 11
      Political Transformation 11
        Political Participation 14
        Rule of Law 20
        Stability of Democratic Institutions 23
        Political and Social Integration 26
      Economic Transformation 30
        Level of Socioeconomic Development 30
        Organization of the Market and Competition 33
        Currency and Price Stability 40
        Private Property 44
        Welfare Regime 47
        Economic Performance 52
        Sustainability 56
      Transformation Management 62
        Level of Difficulty 63
        Management Performance 65
          Steering Capability 65
          Resource Efficiency 69
          Consensus-Building 77
          International Cooperation 83
    Strategic Outlook 86

  Madagascar Government and Politics 90

  Madagascar's political rights Measure 110
    Political Rights and Civil Liberties: 111
    Civil Liberties: 30 / 60 (+2) 115

  Women's Access to Political Leadership in Madagascar: The Value of History and Social Political Activism 121

  Madagascar Election 146

  Madagascar: Measuring the Impact of the Political Crisis 190

Madagascar Political Layout.

Madagascar Political Insider Overview

The former French colony in the Indian Ocean, off the coast of Mozambique with a landmass 1.5 times that of Germany, but with a population of only 20 million, is now facing a huge humanitarian crisis, according to Natascha Paddison, acting Deputy Representative for UNICEF: "The country's health and education systems are not really working, they are crumbling", she says.

Following the 2009 coup d'état by former mayor of Antananarivo, Mr. Marc Ravalomanana was ousted by Andy Rajoelina who is now heading the High Transitional Authority (HTA), the unrecognized government of Madagascar. The unconstitutional change of power by Rajoelina has made an already dire situation much worse: "Following the coup all aid to Madagascar was suspended", explains Paddison, "that is catastrophic for a country where foreign aid accounted for 70 % of the national budget", she continues.

Madagascar is one of the world's poorest countries and has had a negative growth of GDP in the last year; its external debt is now almost 3 billion US dollars. "In the last two years 77 % of the population have been living on less than 1.25 dollars a day", Paddison says. According to a US Congress report Madagascar's infant mortality rate is over 5% and three-quarters of the population is living in rural areas.

"The goal is to have free and fair elections taking place in Madagascar as soon as possible, but that has so far been impossible", says Paddison. "The current government simply has no vested interest in letting free and fair elections take place, there are rumours that they are so embroiled in corruption themselves", she explains. The main political opposition leaders are living in exile in South Africa and France. The political impasse makes humanitarian help very difficult Paddison says and continues, "in 2010 the government cut its health budget by 30% there's no new infrastructure in healthcare being built, no new schools." According to an Amnesty International report for 2011, Madagascan authorities have been violating human rights such as excessive use of force and violence, arbitrary arrests and detentions, limiting freedom of expression and unfair trials.

In addition to its political troubles Madagascar is a country prone to natural disasters like heavy floods and severe drought. "Every year we have 3-4 cyclones that hit Madagascar and they knock down schools and houses and leave people pretty destitute, also in the south we have a lot of droughts and floods, it's not helping the situation," Natascha Paddison explains. In addition Madagascar's biologically diverse fauna is facing ever increasing pressure from deforestation, agricultural production and overgrazing, and desertification and water pollution. Paddison says it is highly likely that the government itself is causing damage to the environment: "There is evidence that there is a lot of illegal foresting going on, in addition there are some "ruling families" that control all of Madagascar's mining for precious stones like diamonds, gold, sapphires, while the population suffers."

This combination of political misrule and volatile weather leaves Madagascar and its people in dire straits. "The problem is that the government is not prioritizing the social sectors. It is channeling the money into its own affairs", says Paddison and adds that the only way forward is to help people directly rather than through government channels: "We have a 60 million dollar trust fund for education that usually goes to the government for dealing with these kinds of problems, but recently this fund has gone to UNICEF. We pay local authorities for health workers and teachers directly

Madagascar Political Transformation

Executive Summary

The year 2013 was a turning point in Madagascar's political history. After almost five years of political crisis following 2009's unconstitutional change of government, which led to a deep governance crisis, international isolation and sanctions, Madagascar succeeded in organizing general elections (presidential and parliamentary), a necessary step toward ending the crisis and restoring international and regional relations. As Madagascar once again possesses elected institutions and is recognized as a potential international and regional partner, the conditions are ripe for an improvement in democratic and economic performance.

However, challenges for these elected institutions remain massive. The country has experienced a decline in most social and economic indicators, and remains one of the poorest countries in the world. Indeed, though a large segment of the population has long experienced frequent disruptions stemming from natural disasters, international economic shocks, malnutrition or sickness, the situation has deteriorated considerably since 2009. Moreover, the five-year transitional period was characterized by institutional decay, widespread corruption and illegal trafficking.

Indeed, the consequences of the crisis are still hampering governance, economic and social progress. Drastic changes in governance mechanisms, the management of resources, social expenditures and political will are needed if the country is to recover fully from the deep impact of the crisis. However, from 2013 to 2015, the country's politics were mainly dominated by the organization of elections and the creation of a new government. Political tensions continued to complicate the political landscape, slowing the creation of the government and the formulation of the strategic plans needed to tackle the society's challenges. Expectations for the new government are high at both the national and international levels, and there is strong pressure to deliver immediate results following the conclusion of the political crisis.

Making a promising beginning, policymakers have set clear political and economic-development objectives through the elaboration of a variety of strategic plans. External expertise and recommendations from international partners and donors have played a strong role in the development of these strategic documents. The donor community is again willing to assist the country, and the government has shown itself open to close collaboration with the international donor community (IMF, World Bank, European Union, U.N. agencies, bilateral donors), despite the imposition of reform requirements as a condition of unlocking aid. Moreover, political attention is invested in the national reconciliation process, with all former and current presidents uniting behind this issue for the first time in the country's history.

Despite these rather positive signs, progress over the last two years has been muted in all areas, creating a general frustration. In terms of economic growth, Madagascar is not yet at the average level for sub-Saharan Africa. By the end of the review period, it was clear that the country would not achieve its Millennium Development Goals (MDGs) by the close of 2015. Moreover, although Madagascar does have assets such as natural resources, land, touristic appeal, a free zone (export-processing zone) for textile manufacturing, and ICT-related services, the country will have to settle its recurrent political unrest, fight corruption, train its workforce, improve its infrastructure and improve its health and education systems before being accepted as a partner deserving of international trust, enabling it to achieve economic growth.

As a consequence of these generally subdued results, as well as the continuing social unrest, the Roger Kolo government was forced to resign on 12 January 2015, before having completed a full year in office. A new government led by Prime Minister Jean Ravelonarivo took office on 25 January 2015, and is expected to put in place policies that will allow for results that can improve democracy and market economy.

History and Characteristics of Transformation

While many African states were created by colonial forces, Madagascar's modern era began with the Merina King Andrianampoinimerina (1787 – 1810), who began the process of taking control of the Highlands, first through the twelve sacred hills of Imerina and then toward the coasts. When the French deposed the monarchy in 1896, the colonial power had merely to take advantage of the administrative system in place. The Merina system of slavery was abolished, but the caste system was adopted in order to develop a new plantation system. Even the system of taxation established by the Merina monarchy was maintained in order to pay for labor and infrastructure development. The Malagasy uprising of 1947 was one of the most violent anywhere in the colonial world, with an estimated 100,000 losing their lives, but it helped bring about the French Loi Cadre of 1956, and ultimately the move to an independent Madagascar on 26 June 1960.

The president of Madagascar's First Republic (1960 – 1972), Philibert Tsiranana, is largely viewed as having remained too close to France. Social movements in the capital led to a peaceful handover to military government. Vice Admiral Didier Ratsiraka adopted a particular brand of scientific socialism in 1975. By 1979, poor economic decisions led to a complete depletion of foreign reserves. Ratsiraka called on the IMF and instead adopted a market-oriented economy.

Political change came in the form of a civil servants' strike that led to the establishment of a transitional government on 31 October 1991. A new constitution was ratified a few months later, and the country's first nominally democratic elections were held in November 1992, bringing Albert Zafy to office. The Zafy period was marked by economic decline, and he was impeached on 26 July 1996 after manipulating a constitutional change and being charged with corruption and abuse of power. The 1996 election was an exercise in banality, with the choice between the disgraced Zafy, the technocratic interim president Norbert Ratsirahonana, and Didier Ratsiraka running as a new kind of democrat. Ratsiraka won, changed the constitution through popular referendum, and set out to consolidate much of the character of the Second Republic.

The 2001 elections gave rise to a conflict between acting president Ratsiraka and Marc Ravalomanana, the mayor of Antananarivo and a self-made millionaire. After six months of social, political and economic conflict, Ravalomanana was recognized as president of the republic. Although he was reelected in 2006, and his administration did usher in economic progress, his domination of both the political and economic spheres led to conflict and political unrest. In 2009, President Ravalomanana relinquished control to a military directorate, who then gave the power to Andry Rajoelina, the mayor of Antananarivo. The latter became president of the so-called High Authority of the Transition. Marc Ravalomanana was forced into exile to Swaziland, and then to South Africa. The unconstitutional change of government was heavily criticized by the African Union (AU) and the Southern African Development Community (SADC), and much of the international community (United States, European Union, etc.) aside from France imposed sanctions. Consequently, Madagascar was deprived of foreign budget support.

In September 2011, 11 political parties signed a roadmap calling for presidential and legislative elections. These elections took place in late 2013, Marc Ravalomanana and Andry Rajoelina both signed an agreement stating they would not stand as candidates. The candidate supported by Rajoelina, Hery Rajaonarimampianina, defeated Ravalomanana's favorite, Jean-Louis Robinson, garnering 53.5% of the presidential vote on 20 December 2013. He was inaugurated on 25 January 2014.

Transformation Status

Political Transformation

While the state has a monopoly on the use of force (army, police, gendarmerie), but Madagascar's security sector has always been weak, having been subject to external influences and instrumentalized by successive heads of state. Poor working conditions within these services, including low pay and a lack of equipment, as well as corruption more generally, have generated conditions for armed violence. The state's monopoly on the use of force has moreover been challenged by bandits (dahalo) in country's south, and by other economic predators mainly in the rural areas where the security forces have colluded with the bandits. Politicization has weakened and divided the security forces. The appointment of 59 generals in December 2014 by new President Hery Rajaonarimampianina can be seen in this light.Some groups are denied full citizenship rights. The outdated Malagasy Nationality Code (1960) prescribes that only those of Malagasy descent are eligible for Malagasy nationality. The application of this concept of nationality, based on a rigorous principle of jus sanguinis, renders country's communities of foreign origin effectively stateless, despite their presence in Madagascar for generations. This includes about 400,000 Indo-Pakistani persons (the so-called karana), between 70,000 and 120,000 Comorians, about 15,000 Chinese, and some 5,000 people of Arab origin. In 2014, discussions aimed at reforming this legislation were opened.

In general, the nation-state is accepted by the major groups in society.

The constitution states that Madagascar is a secular state. However, churches and religious groups such as the Council of Christian Churches in Madagascar (FFKM) have played an important role in politics. The FFKM consists of four churches: the Protestant Church of Jesus Christ in Madagascar (Fiangonan'i Jesoa Kristy eto Madagasikara, FJKM), the Catholic Apostolic Church of Rome (Eglizy Katolika Apostolika Romana, EKAR), the Malagasy Lutheran Church (Fiangonana Loterana Malagasy, FLM), and the Malagasy Episcopal Church (Eklesia Episkopaly Malagasy, EEM).

Religious dogmas have also played an important role in Madagascar's history. The FFKM has been involved in all modern political crises (1991; 2001 – 2002; 2009), and most political leaders use their religion as an instrument of mobilization. In December 2014, the FFKM led the reconciliation process.

This said, the influence of religious dogmas on policy matters such as abortion, same-sex marriage or divorce is small. Laws have passed after secular debate.

Following President Ravalomana's ouster, the state administration fell into a crisis due to the scarcity of resources. Both the quality and quantity of service delivery declined. Basic administrative structures and especially the provision of basic services were further undercut as development aid was considerably reduced. The slow but steady loss of state administrative capacity in all areas has led to increased local and community efforts in selected areas (i.e., schools, security, transportation, water management).

Today, basic administrative structures are present across the country, but remained weakened by the lack of decentralization, and particularly by the absence of fiscal autonomy. The central government does not meet the needs of the many regions. The 2010 constitution defines three levels of decentralized territorial entities (Collectivités territoriales décentralisées), provinces (six), regions (22) and communes (the number of which had not been legally established as of the time of writing). Nevertheless, Madagascar remains a very centralized country, both administratively and fiscally.

As a consequence of these weaknesses, basic state functions are often performed today by national and international organizations.

Political Participation

Madagascar is experiencing an unprecedented crisis following the unconstitutional change of power in March 2009. After the 1972, 1990 and 2001 crises, 2009 is the most serious political crisis facing the country since independence. After various national and international mediation attempts, 11 political parties signed a road map toward new elections (sponsored by the African Union and Southern African Development Community (SADC) with United Nations support) on 16 September 2011. Signatories included the political movements led by former presidents Albert Zafy and Marc Ravalomanana, as well as the president of the High Authority of Transition (HAT), Andry Rajoelina. However, former President Didier Ratsiraka abstained.

The road map put in place an Independent National Electoral Commission for the Transition (Commission Electorale

Nationale Indépendante pour la Transition, CENI-T, Law number 2012-004 of 1 February 2012). The new electoral law changed the voting process to a single-ballot system.

An electoral process supported by the international community was initiated in early 2012 and an electoral calendar foreseeing elections in May and July 2013 was adopted jointly by the CENI-T and international experts. This schedule underwent an initial postponement for technical reasons during a CENI-T conclave on 5 February. Following this delay, the first round of the presidential elections was scheduled for 24 July 24 2013, with the 2nd round paired with the 25 September legislative elections.

On May 3, the Special Electoral Court (Cour Electorale Spéciale) released the list of 41 official candidates for the presidential election of 24 July. This list included the acceptance of applications in violation of legal provisions, including those of Andry Rajoelina, Lalao Ravalomanana (the wife of Marc Ravalomanana) and Didier Ratsiraka. The validation of these applications clearly discredited the Special Electoral Court's claims to impartiality, and created a new political and legal crisis.

The international community opposed these three applications and requested their withdrawal.

A seven-point plan was subsequently developed by the International Contact Group-Madagascar. This included an amendment of the Electoral Code to allow any candidate to withdraw; a reform of the Special Electoral Court; removal of Rajoelina from the list of candidates, the creation of a new list of candidates, the implementation of targeted sanctions, support for the FFKM mediation initiative in compliance with the road map, and support of the electoral process by the international community.

The seven-point plan was implemented between August 8 and 23, and a new timetable was developed jointly by the CENI-T and the United Nations, fixing the first round of the presidential election for 25 October 2013, with the second round paired with the parliamentary elections on 20 December 2013. The new CES validated the candidacy of 33 people, this time excluding Rajoelina, Ratsiraka and Lalao Ravalomanana and five other candidates (Roger Kolo, Jules Etienne Roland, Fleury Rakotomalala, Ny Rado Rafalimanana, Emma Rasolovoahangy). Candidate Dolin Rasolosoa decided to withdraw. Only Roger Kolo and Jules Etienne Roland offered an alternative candidate, in the person of Hery Rajaonarimampianina. The Ravalomanana-led movement threatened to leave the process, but ultimately decided to support Dr. Jean Louis Robinson.

The elections themselves were generally accepted as free and fair, as the major national and international observation missions concluded. As explained earlier, this was the first time in Madagascar's history that neither the incumbent president nor any former ones were on the presidential ballot. Moreover, these were the first elections to be organized by an Independent Electoral Commission with the support of the international community, and the first time that a single ballot sheet was used rather than asking political parties to distribute their individual ballots throughout the country's 20,001 polling stations. This structure helped level the playing field for all candidates, and contributed to the avoidance of fraud. Candidates were given equal amounts of free airtime to present their agendas on public radio and television. Although there were shortcomings in the technical organization of the process, especially with regard to the voter list, as well as major protests by the losing candidates, the results were ultimately accepted and the elected institutions put into place.

The new elected political representatives have considerable formal power to govern. However, their power is relatively weak because of the prevailing power structure. The president does not have the support of a strong political party (his political party, Hery Vaovao Madagasikara, was created only after the elections) and the National Assembly is composed of numerous political parties without a real majority for the president.

Informally, presidents have consistently maintained significant informal networks of power (economic elite, religious elite (FFKM), military elite). This is a necessary condition of maintaining formal power, as these groups have the potential to undermine democratically elected representatives.

The constitution of the Fourth Republic (Article 10) guarantees the freedoms of association and assembly, but obtaining a permit to hold unrestricted events has become more difficult.

A number of demonstrators were arrested in Tamatave in December 2014. The police used excessive force during the protest, resulting in the deaths of two demonstrators. A similar event occurred in Morondava.

In practice, opposition political parties and civil society organizations are often denied permission to engage in protests. In the capital, the police prefecture rarely issues permissions.

This fact helps explains civil society's weakness in holding the elected institutions accountable. As a pressure group, civil society is not strongly structured or well organized, in part because of the limited opportunity to express public disagreement with government policies and practices.

The constitution of the Fourth Republic guarantees freedom of expression. In practice, the media are free to publish a variety of opinions, but the government does not hesitate to call them to order if it considers they have overstepped their role. This means they are often subject to interference or government restrictions, and some journalists consequently practice self-censorship.

On 19 June 2014, the National Assembly adopted a cybercrime law (Law No. 2014-006) that provides for prison sentences for anyone insulting or defaming a state representative online. Under Article 20 of the new law, using print or electronic media to "insult or defame" state representatives will be punishable by two to five years of imprisonment and/or a fine of MGA 2 million to MGA 100 million (€600 to €30,000).

In July 2014, two journalists were held on defamation charges for publishing a reader's letter accusing government ministers of involvement in the trafficking of rosewood. Their arrest came just weeks after a disturbing comment about media freedom by the president. He said there were "limits" to press freedom, and warned journalists to "be on their guard," while the prime minister asked journalists to stop putting "difficult questions" to the president. On July 25, the defamation complaint targeting

Jean-Luc Rahaga and Solo Rabfiringa was withdrawn, and the journalists were released.

Rule of Law

The constitution of the Fourth Republic consists of 168 articles. The state is organized along the three branches of power: the president and his or her government form the executive; the National Assembly and the Senate form the legislature; and the High Constitutional Court, the Courts of Appeal and the lower courts attached to them constitute the judicial power.

The president, who serves as head of state, is elected for a five-year mandate through universal direct suffrage, and can serve no more than two terms. The prime minister is appointed by president, and is nominated by the majority party or group of parties in the National Assembly. The president can also terminate the prime minister's service, either through the resignation of the government, or in the case of grave fault or manifest failure (Article 54 of the constitution).

The separation of powers established by the constitution is weak in practice. The executive is the main power, dominating the other branches. The president holds vast powers; under Article 85, he appoints half the Senate seats, can convene extraordinary sessions of parliament and call for referenda. The personalization of power by successive presidents has undermined checks and balances. An authoritarian power was in place for a long time, hampering the emergence of independent and credible institutions.

The Malagasy judicial system derives from the French tradition. A single judicial system has been in place since independence. The previous system was a bifurcated one with customary courts for most Malagasy and local courts for foreign residents and urbanized Malagasy.

There are three level of courts in today's Malagasy judicial system. First, lower courts handle civil and criminal cases, and can issue limited fines and sentences. Secondly, the Court of Appeals includes a criminal court for cases carrying sentences of five years or more. Finally, the Supreme Court is the country's highest court.

Additionally, the Constitutional High Court reviews whether treaties, laws and ordinances conform with the constitution. Moreover, it rules on disputes related to referendums and presidential or legislative elections, and proclaims the results of the presidential and legislative elections and referendums.

The military courts are organized by civilian magistrates. Its mandate includes issues dealing with national security.

The president serves as formal guarantor of the independence of the judiciary. To this end, he is assisted by a Superior Council of the Magistrature, on which he serves as president, and the minister of justice is vice president. The judiciary remains under the control of the Ministry of Justice, and reports of corruption in the judiciary continue. Efforts are underway to address this problem. The court system has a large backlog of cases, a fact that contributes to excessive investigative detention.

The personalization of power by successive presidents has affected the functioning, transparency and independence of other institutions, especially the judiciary. As a consequence, the Malagasy have lost faith in in the court system. Madagascar ranked 134th out of 144 countries in the World Economic Forum's Global Competitiveness Report 2014 – 2015 with regard to the issue of judicial independence.

Madagascar ratified the United Nations Convention Against Corruption on 22 September 2004, as well as the African Union Convention on Preventing and Combating Corruption on 6 October 2004. Madagascar is also part of the SADC Protocol Against Corruption.

However, the government has not implemented these policies effectively, and corruption remains a serious issue, as does the lack of government transparency.

The inefficiency in sanctioning corrupt public-office holders is due to the lack of independence within the Independent Anticorruption Bureau (BIANCO), political pressure and the power of money. BIANCO lacks sufficient resources, and political interference is evident. A variety of cases has illustrated the widespread impunity for officeholders who break the law, especially with regard to the trafficking of natural resources.

The overall worrisome state of civil rights in Madagascar did not change with the 2013 elections. There are still abuses of power, and restrictions on press freedom and the freedoms of assembly and speech. Significant civil-rights concerns have been associated with the new regime's inability to ensure adherence to the rule of law, resulting in abuses perpetrated by the security forces (for instance in the south with the Coup d'Arrêt operation, and on the east coast in response to the strike against electricity cuts). This has included unlawful killings, and mob violence (on the west coast).

Some media are subject to government censorship, harassment and intimidation, even though the constitution provides for the freedoms of speech and of the press.

Stability of Democratic Institutions
The 2013 elections were a major step forward, but democratic institutions remain weak. Institutions matter less than personal

relationships, and an atmosphere of zero-sum politics continues to exist. This results in both structural and institutional weaknesses.

Political parties' lack of institutionalization (President Rajaonarimampianina did not have a political party before the elections) produces chaotic parliamentary dynamics within the National Assembly. The nomination of the prime minister was disputed. The Party of Andry Rajoelina (MAPAR) and his allies, which controlled a total of 77 seats, claimed the right to nominate the prime minister. However, a new bloc calling itself the Platform for a Presidential Majority (PMP), a coalition of various parties such as the Ravalomanana Movement, the Green Party, Leader Fanilo, Vondrona Politika Miara dia Malagasy Miara Miainga (VPM-MMM), Hiaraka Isika, the MDM and some independents, claimed the right for itself, with a majority of 86 seats.

The High Constitutional Court (HCC) ruled in MAPAR's favor on 18 February 2014. MAPAR nominated Haja Resampa, but this was rejected by the president. The PMP instead nominated Rolland Jules Etienne, but the president was forced to reject him as well as a result of the initial HCC ruling.

President Rajaonarimampianina subsequently decided to change the members of the court, as their mandate had expired in 2010.

He appointed three new members, following the procedure laid out in the constitution (Article 114).

On 27 March 2014, the HCC declared the election of Christine Razanamahasoa (MAPAR) as president of the National Assembly to be unconstitutional. A new president, Jean Max Rakotomamonjy (Leader Fanilo; at this point the only candidate) was elected on 3 May 2014. Christine Razanamahasoa rejected the ruling, saying the HCC did not have the authority to nullify the legislature's internal procedures. On 11 April 2014, the PMP nominated Roger Kolo as prime minister. He was confirmed by Hery Rajaonarimampianina. Ten months after his nomination, popular protests over power cuts and a general failure to provide adequate public services led the prime minister and his cabinet to resign, and the president named a military general, Jean Ravelonarivo, as his new prime minister on 15 January 2015.

The president holds the most power within the Malagasy political system.

Except for some hardliners in the opposition (Comité de l'Opposition Extra-Parlementaire), the government and all significant political actors support the country's democratic institutions. As an example, on 22 January 2015, the Comité de l'Opposition Extra-Parlementaire asked for the dissolution of the

National Assembly, but as the president and the majority of the National Assembly are political allies, the likelihood of any such dissolution is minimal.

This indicates that despite the existence of a certain will to destabilize the institutions, the majority of actors – especially the military and the economic interest groups – accept the elected institutions for the time being.

Since December 2014, the FFKM (Council of Christian Churches in Madagascar) has led a national reconciliation process between Hery Rajaonarimampianina and four former presidents, another important step toward political stabilization.

Political and Social Integration

Madagascar's political institutions are inefficient, partly due to the lack of a stable pattern of political-party organization, which in turn is an expression of the parties' shallow roots in society. Nearly all modern presidents have created their political parties after their elections. Notable exceptions are Philibert Tsiranana's PSD and Albert Zafy's UNDD parties. Didier Ratisraka's AREMA, Marc Ravalomanana's TIM, Andry Rajoelina's TGV and Hery Rajaonarimampianina's Hery Vaovao parties were all created after their leaders were in power. With about 230 registered political parties, the system is highly fragmented. For example, 42 of the parliament's newly elected members, or 29%, were registered either as their own party or as independents. While President Rajaonarimampianina's Hery Vaovao has no sitting parliamentarians, most of the political parties in the National Assembly support him. This situation confirms the winner-takes-all aspect of Malagasy politics, and illustrates the prevailing reluctance to play an opposition role. The absence of public funding continues to make political parties dependent on wealthy individuals who use political parties as a vehicle for their political ambitions.

There are numerous professional associations and other organizations that represent private sector interests and specific industries. These organizations regularly promote dialogue between firms and engage in coordinated policy advocacy. However, private-sector actors argue that few of their policy recommendations are followed. Some discussions were conducted with the government and the National Assembly after the 2013 elections.

There are a total of about 800 associations and NGOs. More than 60% are in the province of Antananarivo, with the provinces of Toamasina and Fianarantsoa also host to a healthy number. According to a 2013 report by the Madagascar National

Institute of Statistics (Instat), most of these are active in the areas of social welfare, health or education. However, only a small number of groups have significant capacity for interest representation. Most are instead groups that are either NGOs funded by donors for a specific community-level purpose, but with limited capacity for representation, or are capital-based groups largely dependent on the funding and activities of their leaders. Organizational capacity therefore remains very low on the average, with limited financial resources, human resources and communication even among core constituents. Another major problem is that some interest groups are politically connected, and are consequently unable to play an effective watchdog role.

There are a few notable exceptions to this general picture. Some faith-based development organizations, such as Sehatra Fanaraha-maso ny Fiainam-pirenena (SeFaFi), have created significant vertical integration and can thus communicate effectively both up and down organizational levels. However, one of this group's members has been nominated to serve as president of the High Constitutional Court.

The Council of Christian Churches of Madagascar still plays a political role. Since December 2014, it has been leading the national reconciliation process.

According to the most recent Afrobarometer survey, published in January 2014 and taking into account data from 2013, the population's trust in existing institutions is relatively weak, a phenomenon explained by the high level of corruption. This mistrust has increased since the previous Afrobarometer surveys (2005 and 2008), as corruption (perceived and real) has also increased, especially during the political crisis beginning in 2009.

In the most recent survey, about 50% of respondents declared that they had confidence in institutions such as the presidency, police and army, while about 40% said they trusted the electoral commission and the lower courts. Less than 30% said they had confidence in the state tax bureaucracy or the political parties (including the ones in power and those in opposition).

Approval of a democratic system had fallen compared to previous Afrobarometer surveys, though the most recent data still dates from before the 2013 general elections. While a majority still said they supported democratic principles, 9% of the respondents said they were in favor of a single-party system centralizing power at the presidential level, while 20% said they were in favor of the army taking power. Only 39% of respondents identified democracy as preferable to any other form of governance. Similarly, concerning the quality of democratic performance, only 29% of the respondents were of the opinion that Madagascar was a full democracy, whereas 32%

declared that Madagascar was not a democracy at all or was one with major shortcomings. A full 40% failed to respond to this question, which suggests a general apathy regarding political matters.

Survey data on social capital and solidarity among the citizens are limited. However, the concept of social capital may be defined in Malagasy society as "fihavanana," which can be translated as solidarity, mutual understanding and respect, social justice and peaceful cohabitation. This is generally present within Malagasy culture. However, observers note that solidarity and trust among citizens have been affected by the almost five years of political crisis, deepening social and economic rifts. On the other hand, the weakened presence of state services has pushed people to rely on solidarity as a means of survival. While self-organized groups fulfil this role, no quantitative data exist to confirm an increase of this type of group. In general, trust and solidarity tend to be organized along family, regional, and religious lines, and are structured by the strong presence of community traditions.

Economic Transformation
Level of Socioeconomic Development
The United Nations Development Program (UNDP) ranks Madagascar 155th out of 187 in its Human Development Index

(24 out of 52 in Africa). Madagascar falls into the category of low human development, and as of the time of writing, it was evident that it would not achieve most of the U.N. Millennium Development Goals (MDGs) by 2015. Poverty has sharply increased; indeed, the World Bank estimates that more than 92% of Malagasy live under the $2-per-day poverty line, up from 89% in 2001. Moreover, 43% live below the $1.25-per-day extreme-poverty line, up from a low of 26.5% in 2005. Farmers (between 79% and 86% of households) are among the poorest individuals, followed by the self-employed (43%). The poorest regions are Androy and Atsimo-Atsinanana, both situated in rural areas.

Despite crisis-related aid, as many as 600,000 children have left school. Poor parents have had to shoulder a heavy proportion of the costs for their children's schooling due to a lack of government funding.

Economic indicators		2005	2010	2013	**2014**
GDP	$ M	5039.3	8729.9	10613.5	**10593.1**
GDP growth	%	4.6	0.3	2.4	**3.0**
Inflation (CPI)	%	18.5	9.2	5.8	**6.1**

		2005	2010	2013	2014
Unemployment	%	2.6	3.6	3.6	-

Economic indicators		2005	2010	2013	**2014**
Foreign direct investment	% of GDP	1.7	9.3	5.3	-
Export growth	%	2.2	3.1	32.4	-
Import growth	%	-8.8	-6.1	10.1	-
Current account balance	$ M	-694.7	-887.7	-622.1	-
Public debt	% of GDP	86.4	31.9	34.0	**34.7**
External debt	$ M	3521.1	2699.3	2848.7	-
Total debt service	$ M	79.6	60.4	69.6	-
Cash surplus or deficit	% of GDP	-4.6	-0.9	-	-
Tax revenue	% of GDP	10.1	9.8	-	-
Government consumption	% of GDP	9.2	10.6	8.6	-
Public expnd. on education	% of GDP	3.8	-	2.1	-
Public expnd. on health	% of GDP	2.5	2.7	2.6	-
R&D expenditure	% of GDP	0.18	0.11	-	-
Military expenditure	% of GDP	1.1	0.7	0.7	**0.7**

Organization of the Market and Competition

Malagasy political culture is liberal, and some parts of the country have a long history of market integration. For instance, the country is the world's largest supplier of vanilla, and the vanilla industry of the northeastern coast has remained a significant economic and political force since the colonial period. There are nonetheless significant market distortions. The vanilla coast is one of the world's wettest inhabited regions and infrastructure remains a challenge. Vanilla growers remain largely at the mercy of organized vanilla companies and a scandalously ruthless, largely Chinese middleman market. As a result, growers commonly receive less than 5% of the international market price for their product.

This dichotomy between a market culture and opportunity on the one hand and significant structural barriers on the other is characteristic of the ongoing challenge Madagascar has faced with regard to market fundamentals. The World Bank's Doing Business index ranked Madagascar 163rd in 2015, down from 157th place only a year ago. In this regard, it is very close to the sub-Saharan Africa average. This places it among countries struggling with market-economy issues, but above the direst cases. The currency has long operated on a floating exchange basis with relatively little political interference. The informal market is relatively small (estimated at approximately 17% of the national economy by one scholarly study). However, approximately 65% of the labor force in Madagascar's capital of Antananarivo was estimated to have worked in the informal economy in 2011, and that figure might have increased further in the wake of the political and economic crisis.

Improvement has been evident in some areas. For example, it has become easier since 2005 to trade across borders, pay taxes and register property. International investors have been given significant liberties to invest, while nascent capital markets have helped domestic entrepreneurs to flourish. In the Doing Business 2015 report, Madagascar was ranked 37th in the world in terms of the ease of starting a business (down from 33rd in Doing Business 2014). By comparison, Mauritius was ranked 29th, and Rwanda 112nd. It takes eight days to start a business in Madagascar (compared to six in Mauritius and 6.5 in Rwanda).

Nonetheless, structural barriers remain and even have worsened. Insolvency has reached crisis proportions, and addressing that problem has become more difficult. The formal sector has improved structurally, but has actually shrunk. As industries that face a large tax burden have grown, the percentage of small and large businesses that have exited the formal sector for the informal sphere has increased.

Madagascar has recently become an industrial-mining country. Since 2009, permits for new mining activities have proliferated, with loose oversight driving new employment, but with investments from new international partners having little transparency. The illegal timber trade has increased dramatically over the same period. Finally, the textile industry has been badly hampered by the political crisis, as well as by the loss of African Growth and Opportunity Act (AGOA) trade preferences in 2009 following the country's unconstitutional change in power, as the country no longer met the AGOA criteria regarding political pluralism and the rule of law. Recognizing Madagascar's return to political pluralism after internationally observed elections in late 2013, the United States announced the restoration of Madagascar's AGOA eligibility on 27 June 2014. This represents a good opportunity for the textile industry.

During the 1990s and particularly the 2000s, Madagascar saw a large sell-off of state-owned enterprises. For example, the state companies producing sugar (SIRAMA) and cotton (HASYMA) were privatized. However, the state remains a shareholder in hotel operations (Carlton), fishing (Nosy Be fishery), textiles (Cotona, FITIM), wood (Fanalamanga), the production and distribution of beverages (Star), air travel (Air Madagascar), telephony (Telma) and the exploitation of granite and marble resources (MAGRAMA). The presence of the state in these areas helps to explain the lack of competition these firms have enjoyed over the years.

The state has a monopoly in the electricity and water industry (JIRAMA), which provides irregular power supply in many regions, particularly in remote coastal provinces.

Several monopolies or cartels have been consolidated in areas such as the production and distribution of food (dairy products, oils, flours) and beverages (beer and non-alcoholic drinks). There is evidence of collusion between the political and the economic elite. These competition-dampening monopolies have helped maintain relatively high prices for consumers, particularly for the poorest, and discourage technological development.

There are few antitrust laws within the private sector (with the exception of Law No. 2005-020). However, as of the time of writing, a new law was slated for adoption and a competition council was in the works.

Madagascar belongs to the World Trade Organization (WTO). It is also member of several regional groupings, including the Common Market for Eastern and Southern Africa (COMESA), the Southern African Development Community (SADC) and the Indian Ocean Commission (IOC), but has little trade with them.

The European Union remains the country's largest trading partner, accounting for 24% of imports and 53% of exports. China is the second-largest point of origin for imports (13%), while the United States is the second-largest export destination (24%).

As a WTO member, Madagascar is required to implement that body's Trade Related Investment Measures (TRIMS). In general, performance requirements are not imposed as conditions for establishing or maintaining investments, with the exception of the Export Processing Zones (EPZ) regime. In this case, firms must export 95% of their output in order to qualify for EPZ investment incentives. Projects owned by foreign or local investors can benefit from EPZ tax exemptions if they fit into the following categories: 1) investment in export-oriented manufacturing industries; 2) development or management of industrial free zones; or 3) provision of services to EPZ companies.

The government has established free industrial zones (ZFI) to revive exports, in particular in the clothing manufacturing sector. Equipment and other import materials are used in this type of zone are exempt from custom duties. Moreover, most of the products can be imported without an import license.

According to the country's central bank, foreign direct investment inflows amounted to $809 million in 2011 and $894 million in 2012. This increase is partially attributable to an increase in banks' capital holdings, which required them to borrow money from overseas parent companies or from foreign banks, as well as to several major loans taken out by telecommunications companies from abroad.

From January to August of 2014, the trade balance improved compared to the same period of the previous year, due to a slowdown in imports (-2%) and an increase in exports of 7.6%. This imports decline was influenced by a reduction in imported capital goods due to the low level of investment. Invoices for the purchase of energy and raw materials have stabilized compared to the previous year. Export volumes have risen primarily due to exports of mining products and textiles. Non-mining exports had fallen by 4% compared with the 2013 level.

Until fairly recently, the Malagasy banking system was composed of a central bank and six commercial banks. However, the number of financial institutions has increased over the past five years, reaching 11 banks, six non-bank financial institutions (NBFIs) and 31 microfinance institutions. However, a large proportion of the country's banking assets are concentrated within three banks, reflecting the lack of competition. Total financial-sector assets totaled 25.5% of GDP in late 2011.

A leasing company, Equipbail-Madagascar, two mutualist financial institutions, the Adefi and CECAM, and a non-mutualist financial institution, SIPEM, round out the Malagasy banking system.

Banking law No. 95-030 was adopted on 22 February 1996, dealing with issues related to the operation of financial establishments and commercial banks. The Banking and Financial Supervision Commission (CSBF) oversees banks and financial establishments, and must provide operation permits to commercial banks.

Only about 5% of the population uses banks in Madagascar. The quality of bank portfolios was damaged by the crisis, making it difficult for banks to honor commitments. According to the central bank, bad loans represented 14.4% of gross credit in 2012. This figure had risen to MGA 354.9 billion by the end of June 2013, for a 2.8% increase since the end of 2012. While banks had an MGA 118.9 billion surplus over their required reserves by the end of 2012, they lent little to businesses, particularly over the medium or long terms, in large part due to the high political risks. The volume of long-term loans decreased between 2012 and 2011, accounting for just 10.5% of gross credit at the end of 2012. No reforms of financial regulations have been implemented in recent years, largely due to the political crisis.

Financial markets in Madagascar are relatively rudimentary, and the bank penetration rate is very low. This could be explained in part by high interest rates, strong requirements for collateral and guarantees, limited competition among banks, and a reluctance to finance foreign trade or working capital even when loans are secured by letters of credit. In general, financing is expensive and difficult to access. Local firms are confronted with numerous constraints, making expansion almost impossible. One of these limiting factors is the difficulty in increasing working capital through bank borrowing. Banks argue that many prospective borrowers neither have reliable and transparent balance sheets nor engage in long-term deposits, which complicates long-term financing.

Currency and Price Stability

Madagascar is not part of any monetary union. The central bank is responsible for guaranteeing the stability of the local currency in the country and abroad. The bank's interventions on currency markets has kept the ariary relatively steady against major currencies. There was some fluctuation between December 2012 and 2013, with its nominal value falling 3.5% against the euro and rising 0.8% against the dollar. As a consequence of this relative stability, combined with weak internal demand and ongoing fuel subsidies, annual inflation rates were held to 5.8% in 2012 and 6.9% in 2013. However, the cost of staples, especially rice, increased during the period of review following bad harvests, and in order to keep prices down, the government imported some 400,000 tons of rice in 2013.

Monetary aggregates have been kept broadly in check, and inflation did not passed the single-digit level during the period. After peaking at 16.4% in 2011, broad money growth decreased rapidly to 5.5% in 2013. While subdued demand kept credit to the private sector growing more or less in line with nominal GDP through 2012, it accelerated in 2013 mainly due to overdrafts, including those related to imports of petroleum products, and to a lesser extent medium-term (working capital) and long-term (working capital and construction financing) borrowing. The banking sector remains reasonably profitable and liquid.

Macroeconomic stability has been maintained through drastic budgetary adjustments that have undermined the government's ability to provide basic services, and have also restrained economic recovery.

Following the 2013 elections, the World Bank regularized its operations in Madagascar. Similarly, in June 2014, a $47 million rapid credit facility was promised by the International Monetary Fund (IMF), with the goals of rebuilding macroeconomic stability through economic and structural policies and measures, providing a favorable environment for inclusive growth and poverty reduction, and strengthening the capacity of the Malagasy government. That same month, Madagascar again became eligible for favorable trade treatment under the African Growth and Opportunity Act (AGOA), which will stimulate growth in the textile industry and help increase exports to the United States.

Government spending increased by 2.9% of GDP in the supplementary budget of August 2014. Emphasis here was placed on investment, including road rehabilitation, new classrooms and agricultural infrastructure. Consequently, the share devoted to current (rather than capital) expenditure has been reduced, though not substantially. The government also increased its social spending, in part by regularizing the employment status of some of the "community teachers" (Enseignants FRAM) working in public schools. The number of such teachers had increased rapidly during the transition period, as they were hired as replacements for retiring teachers or to staff the new schools being constructed to meet the needs of Madagascar's growing young population.

Around 40% of the increased spending was allocated to transfers and subsidies, including fuel subsidies, and for partial clearance of existing payment arrears and the prevention of future such arrears.

The supplementary budget provides that the additional spending would be sustained in equal measures by additional tax revenues and renewed budget support from international donors, for a total amount of 2.2% to 2.9% of GDP.

The 2015 budget was passed by parliament in December 2014. The macroeconomic policy framework has been firmed up as a result of the IMF's recent Article IV consultation mission (29 October – 11 November 2014). In 2014, the current account deficit is projected to have narrowed to about 2% of GDP, thanks to growing mineral exports, decreasing food-import needs, and lower-than-anticipated international oil prices. Growing credit demand prompted an increase in domestic interest rates, raising the cost of domestic budgetary financing. As a consequence, the government increased its statutory advances from the central bank.

In 2014, expenditure in high-priority sectors such as education and health remained too low, a fact partially explained by still-weak tax-revenue collection. A number of ongoing demands, including the need to finance fuel subsidies, public enterprises (such as the JIRAMA public power and water utility) and the underfunded civil-service pension fund have placed the budget under pressure. However, measures are being taken to strengthen public financial management. For example, policymakers have begun to clear domestic budgetary arrears, have developed a plan to shore up JIRAMA's finances, and have adopted a prioritized action plan.

In general, Madagascar continues to face complex challenges including weak institutions and governance, binding resource constraints, vulnerability to shocks, and the urgent need to reverse recent deterioration in a number of development indicators.

Private Property

Private-property rights are protected within the Malagasy legal system, which is inspired by French civil law. Malagasy commercial law is mostly formed by the country's Code of Commerce and associated laws, which are reportedly applied in a non-discriminatory manner. A bankruptcy law has been in place since 1996, and is included in the Code of Commerce. The Malagasy judicial system has the reputation of being slow, complex, opaque and subject to corruption.

The government accepts binding international arbitration of investment disputes between foreign investors and the state under the privatization law. The Malagasy Arbitration and Mediation Center (CAMM) was created in 2000 as a private organization to promote and facilitate the use of arbitration to resolve commercial disputes and decrease reliance on an overburdened court system. As a result, many private contracts now include arbitration clauses.

Madagascar is a signatory to the International Center for the Settlement of Investment Disputes (ICSID) Convention, as well as the New York Convention of 1958 on the Recognition and Enforcement of Foreign Arbitral Awards. Madagascar has been a member of the Multilateral Investment Guarantee Agency (MIGA) since 1989.

Despite legal advances, the prohibition on land ownership by foreigners remains controversial and problematic. A system of long-term leases (up to 99 years) was established to address the issue in 2008, following the adoption of investment law 2007-036. However, there have been long delays and few successes so far with regard to actually approving land leases for foreigners. The new investment law grants land and property to certain companies registered in Madagascar. Since 2006, the Economic Development Board of Madagascar (EDBM) has been the issuer of authorization documents. The EDBM is intended to bridge public and private interests and facilitate investment.

However, land leases have become one of the most politically controversial issues in Madagascar. Conflicts exist around mining interests, and large-scale foreign-led agricultural operations are often seen as benefiting a small urban elite at the expense of the majority rural poor.

Despite the improvements brought by the 2013 elections, Madagascar's business environment remains troubled. The recent crisis (2009 – 2013) disrupted the country's positive growth trajectory and the economic reforms adopted during the Ravalomanana era (particularly investment law 2007-036 and the Export Processing Zones law 2007-038).

Private companies experienced weak performance during fiscal 2010 through 2013. The real growth rate in annual turnover was a low 2.3% during this period, compared to 9.3% in countries with a similar level of income, and the overall employment growth rate was effectively zero. As of the end of fiscal year 2012, businesses in Madagascar were operating well below full capacity (63%), at a rate lower than the average in other countries in Africa (70%) or in low-income countries more generally (almost 72%).

Madagascar again lost ground in the World Bank's Doing Business 2015 report, dropping six ranks in the overall ranking for ease of doing business to land at 163rd place out of 189 countries.

According to the World Bank's 2013 Enterprise Surveys, the greatest threats to private companies' operations in Madagascar are associated with access to financial services, the growing informal sector, tax rates, corruption, political instability and the unreliability of electricity supply. Isolated from the world's main economic centers and global supply chains, Madagascar also suffers from a lack of competition and an incomplete liberalization of national airspace, both of which mute the country's growth potential. In addition, the state monopoly in the energy sector stifles the manufacturing sector – especially for industries located outside of the capital – and restricts investments in other sectors of the economy such as fishing, tourism and agribusiness.

A process of privatization began in 2001, but has slowed in recent years.

Welfare Regime
The question of the existence of formal and/or informal social safety nets has to be interpreted in the context of data on general living conditions. According to the UNDP, Madagascar's Human Development Index score in 2013 was 0.498. The country was ranked 155th out of 187 countries in this regard. The World

Bank indicates that more than 92% of the population lives on less than $2 a day, and poverty rates have sharply increased in recent years, especially during the political crisis.

The crisis has also had an impact on public social expenditure in areas such as health care and education. Several health care centers have closed, and more and poor parents have had to shoulder a significant proportion of the cost of their children's schooling due to a lack of government funding. As many as 600,000 children have had to drop out of school as a result Acute malnutrition among children has increased in some areas by more than 50%. All of these events threaten the future and well-being of the next generation, and have ensured that Madagascar would not achieve its MDGs by 2015.

According to the World Bank, public expenditures for social protection remain extremely low. Since 2009, these have consisted almost exclusively of payments into a public pension fund, a fact that has sharply reducing expenditures for social safety-net programs.

In May 2014, the new government organized an international forum on social protection, inviting national and international experts, and representatives of non-governmental organizations and development partners working in social-protection-related activities. Subsequently, a social-protection policy-development process was launched. The World Bank is supporting the preparation of a new social-safety-net project for the poorest households, including a conditional cash transfer program for extremely poor families. This project has two objectives: to provide the poorest families with short-term income support while encouraging their children's school enrollment and attendance; and to promote the spread of nutritious food and eating habits, particularly for children. The project also includes a short-term employment program for households affected by disasters, so they do not have to sell their assets to cope with crises.

As of the time of writing, 5,000 households from Betafo (in the Vakinankaratra region) were participating in a pilot program launched by President Hery Rajaonarimampianina on 29 September 2014.

A total of 16,000 students have benefited from a family grant (Vatsin'Ankohonana) program being implemented by the Development Intervention Fund (FID) in collaboration with the Ministry of Population, Social Protection and Women's Promotion; the Ministry of Education; and the National Nutrition Office (ONN). As of the time of writing, the program was expected to be extended through July 2015, taking into account the evaluation and lessons learned from the pilot program.

These initiatives have to been seen against a general situation in which safety nets formally exist (pension, health insurance, etc.), but often fail to reach the poorest and most vulnerable portions of the population.

Legal and constitutional provisions guarantee ethnic, racial, ethnic and gender equity. However, the achievement of equality of opportunity is still a challenge in practice.

Madagascar scores a 3.5 (out of 6) on the World Bank's Country Policy and Institutional Assessment (CPIA) gender-equality rating (2013). In comparison to former parliaments in which women were strongly underrepresented (with less than an 8% share before 2009, and 17.5% in the transitional legislature), the National Assembly elected in 2013 shows an increase in the number of women legislators (23%). In the current government under Prime Minister Jean Ravelonarivo, six of 30 ministers are women. The presidency of the Electoral Management Body is also held by a woman.

However, traditional, cultural, social and economic constraints still prevent women from having overall equal opportunities. The difficulty for women in inheriting land and property is a prime example of gender inequality. In some regions, depending on local ethnic and kinship norms, women have difficulties acquiring land. Early marriage is common, particularly in rural areas, and violence against women is widespread among some ethno-cultural groups.

World Bank figures show no significant differences between school enrollment figures among men and women. The general literacy rate in Madagascar is below the average in Sub-Saharan Africa, and access to secondary and tertiary education remains limited for the vast majority of the population. However, the difference between literacy rates for men and women is just 5.8%. This may help explain the effectively equal labor-force participation rate for women and men (with women making up 49.5% of the total labor force).

According to the World Bank, women's labor-market earnings are not as high as those of men when controlling for various other factors.

Inequality in terms of ethnicity, religion and political preference is a less well-documented topic, and indeed as a rather hidden, subtle and sensitive reality. Although no systematic exclusion on the basis of these characteristics exists, there is evidence that ethnic and regional origin play a role in access to education, employment and the market. In the capital, the Merina-Côtier divide runs through the political, societal and employment spheres. The Merina population has privileged access to education, employment and public office. This is explained in part by the strong centralization of all services and infrastructure in the capital city, which complicates access for the people from the coast.

With regard to political preference, membership in or at least association with the party in power seems necessary in order to have access to high-level employment.

Economic Performance

Madagascar is a country with huge potential human and natural resources. Before the crisis, Madagascar grew at an average of 5% a year; however, economic growth was just 1.9% in 2012 and 2.6% in 2013. Economic growth is largely driven by extractive industries, agro-industry, banking, transport, livestock and fisheries. During the crisis, critical budgetary adjustments improved macroeconomic stability, but prevented the government from providing basic services and ultimately restrained economic recovery. Following the 2013 elections, there were early signs of an economic recovery in 2014, with growth for the year estimated at 3% and the inflation rate falling below 7% in December. The current account deficit is projected to have narrowed to about 2% of GDP in 2014, driven by growing mineral exports, decreasing food-import needs and lower-than-anticipated international oil prices. Growing credit demand prompted an increase in domestic interest rates and raised the cost of domestic budgetary financing, leading the government to increase statutory advances from the central bank.

Given the still-weak tax-revenue collection, spending on high-priority areas such as education and health continued to be constrained in 2014. The need to finance fuel subsidies, public enterprises (such as JIRAMA, the national water and electricity company) and the underfunded civil-service pension fund has added to budgetary pressures. However, the government has begun to clear domestic budgetary arrears, began development of a plan to shore up JIRAMA's finances, and adopted a prioritized action plan for strengthening public financial management.

The National Development Plan (NDP) 2015 – 2019 forecasts growth of 5% in 2015, 7% in 2016, 9% in 2017 and double-digit growth in 2018. An interim plan including the president's Emergency Program for the period 2015 – 2016 is contained in the NDP.

The NDP focuses on five strategic areas: i) governance, rule of law, security, decentralization, democracy and national reconciliation; ii) preservation of macroeconomic stability and support for development; iii) inclusive growth and; iv) human capital; and v) enhancement of natural capital.

The primary sector, which accounts for approximately 30% of GDP, should benefit from government measures intended to increase rice yields. Agricultural production is nevertheless highly vulnerable to locust invasions and climatic conditions that impact harvests on a regular basis. Mineral production, notably nickel and cobalt started in 2013, will continue, together with the exploitation of the Tsimiroro oil field that began in 2014. The textile and clothing sector will be revitalized with the reopening of the U.S. market to Malagasy products and the slight upturn in European demand. Services (55% of GDP), particularly tourism, should remain strong, but the enduring political uncertainties as well as the lack of real strength in economic growth in Europe will hold back any increase in tourism revenue.

Inflation should slow in 2015 thanks to a lower rate of growth in agricultural products. However, a reduction in fuel subsidies, if actually implemented by the government, could hamper efforts to hold down inflation.

Public spending is likely to rise in 2015. Madagascar will gradually address the domestic payments arrears accumulated over a number of years, which are estimated by the IMF to total 2% of GDP. The financial situation of JIRAMA, the source of part of the unpaid public debt, is also a heavy burden on the budget. The government expects the resumption of the international aid suspended after the 2009 coup d'état to provide the funding for its investment spending. The United States and the European Union indicated their agreement in principle to resuming aid following the signature of an agreement between the Malagasy government and the IMF in June 2014. However, payment of the aid is conditional on the finalization of the NDP and the stabilization of the political situation. Cuts in subsidies, increases in tax revenues due to increased mining production, and reforms intended to improve tax collection should help to prevent any serious further deterioration in public finances.

The country's public debt is essentially domestic due to the problems in accessing external markets in recent years. The concessionary nature of the loans the country may be granted once the flow of aid resumes should not seriously increase the country's debt burden.

The current account deficit is expected to stabilize in 2015. Clothing exports will benefit from the gradual economic recovery in the European Union, Madagascar's main trading partner, as well as from the United States' decision to restore the country's eligibility for the Africa Growth and Opportunity Act (AGOA) program granting preferential access by specific African countries to the U.S. market. With the completion of the mining-, oil- and gas-development projects, imports of capital goods are slowing. The need to import food, in particular rice, should ease thanks to improved local harvests. The slowdown in world raw-material prices will also help. The repatriation of profits from extraction activities will continue to have an impact on the balance of payments. Because of continuing uncertainties in the political situation, FDI will remain at a low level.

Sustainability

Natural capital represents 49% of Madagascar's total wealth. In this regard, natural capital can be deemed to include i) forest land that produces timber (roundwood and fuel wood), non-timber forest products, and bioprospecting; ii) protected areas; ii) agricultural land, including cropland and pastureland; and iii) fisheries.

Madagascar accounts for more than 5% of the world's biodiversity, about 90% of it endemic.

Within the African region, Madagascar is the second most vulnerable country to natural disasters. The country's vulnerability is a function both of high exposure levels due to its geographic position, and its low adaptive capacity, which is driven by high rates of poverty and unsustainable land and natural-resource usage.

Several programs aimed at combating environmental damage have been adopted, including an environmental charter, a national environment policy, a national strategy for clean development and a national action plan for adapting to climate change.

The crisis, which weakened governance and regulation and diminished control of domestic security, has increased the incidence of rosewood smuggling and the threat to endangered species.

Progress has been made towards the MDG of ensuring environmental sustainability, according to the 2012/13 national survey of MDG progress. The pace of deforestation has been reduced by 75% in the past 20 years; in 1990, Madagascar had 11 million hectares of forest and 11 million people, whereas there are currently 9 million hectares of forest and 20 million people. New protected areas (11% of the country) have been created. In 2003, Madagascar had 1.7 million hectares protected, while at the 2014 World Parks Congress in Sydney, Hery Rajoanirimampianina said that Madagascar now has a little under 7 million hectares of protected areas.

Nonetheless, environmental protection is hampered by weak institutional capacity. The Ministry of Environment and Forests' (MEF) effectiveness in managing environmental issues is compromised by internal conflicts, resource constraints and limited technical capacity. There is also duplication and ambiguity between the roles allocated to external organizations such as the Office National pour l'Environnement (ONE), which serves as the country's environmental regulator; and Madagascar National Parks (MNP), which is responsible for ensuring the protection of ecosystems and species, promoting research and environmental education, and managing ecotourism activities in national parks.

Two trust funds operate in the environmental sector – the Foundation for Protected Areas and Biodiversity (tasked with providing a secure and sustainable source of financing to the existing protected-area network, and with supporting the creation of new protected areas) and the Foundation Tavy Meva (focused on supporting environmental activities at the local community level).

The legal framework governing environmental protection in Madagascar has been characterized by rapid evolution and a largely reactive approach to the development of legislation. On the whole, it is highly fragmented and incoherent, both within and across legislative instruments.

The administration of education runs vertically in parallel with governing bodies across eight levels, from the Ministry of Higher

Education and Scientific Research, through regional directors of national education (Directeurs Régionaux de l'Éducation Nationale, DREN), local CISCOs (circonscription scolaire), and down to the schools. The private sector plays an important role, with faith-based and independent schools subject to national instructional and examination guidelines. The majority of teachers used to be civil servants. Today, nearly two-thirds of teachers are currently "community teachers" (Fikambanan'ny Ray Amandrenin'ny Mpianatra (FRAM) teachers) with little or no training, and who are hired and funded by parent associations. The system is generally well organized and pervasive, but the challenges of ensuring funding, training, oversight and payment through the official system have become acute.

The academic year begins in October and ends in July, and the official primary-school entrance age is six. The system is structured so that the primary school cycle lasts five years, lower secondary lasts four years, and upper-secondary lasts three years. Madagascar has a total of 5,808,000 pupils enrolled in primary and secondary education. Of these pupils, about 4,403,000 (76%) are enrolled in primary education. During the 2009 – 2013 period, despite crisis-related aid, the number of school-age children not attending school increased, possibly by more than 600,000. Fewer than half of the students who begin primary education reach grade five, and learning outcomes are declining overall (e.g., a 19% point drop in mathematics scores).

The per pupil expenditure (PPE) as a percentage of per capita GDP in primary education is 7%, lower than the median primary-level PPE for low-income countries as a whole, which is 9%. In Madagascar, the primary-level PPE is lower than the secondary-level PPE. The pupil-teacher ratio (PTR) at the primary level is 43.1, meaning that on average there is one teacher for every 43.1 primary school students. This is lower than the median primary-level PTR for low-income countries, which is 44. In Madagascar, the PTR in primary is higher than the PTR in secondary.

In order to optimize the allocation of public expenditure, the 2014 Supplementary Budget Law increased spending on infrastructure and essential services, and increased expenditures related to education (+ 5.5%) compared to the 2014 Initial Budget Act. In the 2015 Budget Law, the social sector will account for 32.6% of the

Public Investment Program budget. This sector will primarily support activities such as providing school supplies, further integrating and reintegrating school-age children, supplying desks and benches, building new classrooms, creating new schools, and supplying them with new equipment and tools (high schools and vocational-training centers).

Madagascar's tertiary-education sector is one of the least developed in the world, and is far behind the average for sub-Saharan Africa. The public sector includes six universities, four senior technology institutes and a national distance-learning center. The private sector includes a growing number of poorly documented institutions that lack coherent framework authorization, accreditation and quality assurance. During the 2000 – 2011 period, the total number of students at the national level increased from 32,156 to 85,548, or from 199 to 385 students per 100,000 inhabitants. The enrollment rate is extremely low, and heavily concentrated in Antananarivo. The six public universities had a total of 52,028 students; the University of Antananarivo accounted 47% of these, and the University of Toamasina another 22%.

The country has not quite reached gender parity, although the proportion of female students has increased slightly to 48.2%.

The number of permanent teachers has not risen in parallel with the student population.

Eight public research centers employ 300 researchers and engineers. Programs here address issues of agricultural production and rural development, health, biodiversity and environmental management, technological innovation, and nuclear technology. Due to lack of funding, no recruitment has taken place in the last decade, and equipment is badly out of date. A national research strategy was published in 2013, structured around four areas: defining research priorities to meet the needs of the country's social and economic development and its environmental constraints; creating a national research agency tasked with defining priorities and evaluation; developing international partnerships; and guaranteeing sufficient public funding.

The current situation is the result of long-term underinvestment and inadequate governance of the higher-education sector. In 2012, public expenditure on higher education was MGA 82 billion, compared to MGA 85 billion the previous year, even though enrollments in public institutions increased by 12.5%. This amounted to 0.3% of GDP, or 12.8% of total public expenditure on education, as compared to 16.8% in 2006. Public spending for research amounted to MGA 10.5 billion, or 0.04% of the state budget in 2012, a decrease from 0.05% in 2007. Most of the budget goes to salaries and student scholarships. As a consequence, educational resources and investment received little funding.

Transformation Management

Level of Difficulty

Structural constraints on governance are high. According to a 2013 World Bank report, existing structural constraints have been exacerbated by the 2009 political crisis, which has lasted for almost 5 years. As an example, poverty has increased significantly, resulting in 92% of the population living under the poverty line. This qualifies the country as one of the poorest in the world. Other intensifying structural constraints include infrastructural deficiencies (roads, electricity and water provision, communication), education and the lack of a skilled labor force (less than 15% of the labor force has a secondary education, and only 3.4% of workers have a tertiary education). Moreover, natural disasters (cyclones, locust invasions), diseases (plague), and the country's isolated geographical position further complicate management performance. Even the return of elected government institutions in 2013 failed to result in improved living conditions after a year, forcing the new prime minister to resign. Structural constraints thus have a real impact on political performance and stability.

In general, civil society is rather weak in Madagascar. Although many associations and NGOs exist on paper, their actions are limited in terms of impact, especially in terms of playing a watchdog or lobbying role with regard to government institutions. The most recent Afrobarometer survey indicates that few citizens are active members of an association or community group (only 17%, compared to an average of 37% over 23 African countries). Among the factors that weaken civil society are politicization; the lack of coordination or collaboration between different associations due to competition for limited resources (especially during the political crisis); and a lack of social rooting on the part of organizations' leaderships, which often acting in their own interests instead of the general interest. However, during the 2013 elections, civil-society organizations coordinated voter-education and election-observation activities, and created nationwide platforms to increase their impact.

Malagasy society is structured by several cleavages of varying type: political, social, ethnic and religious. However, these cleavages do not lead to widespread violence or open, violent conflict. For example, the 2013 electoral process was characterized by political tensions that held the potential to erupt into violent confrontation. However, no open conflict occurred, and elections were conducted in a relatively peaceful environment. One of the reasons is that broad popular mobilization and demonstrations in support of political parties or candidates (or to protest specific issues) have become more difficult, as illustrated by the 2013 Afrobarometer survey. Only 10% of respondents said they had participated in this type of event, with 80% saying they would never take part in a protest or use violence for a political cause. However, social and economic conditions (lack of electricity, lack of payment of scholarships at university level, civil-servant salaries; etc.) have begun mobilizing people, often triggering violent repression in response.

The current reconciliation exercise between current and former presidents illustrates the existence of political cleavages, but has had little impact on a general population that has distanced itself from the political sphere.

Management Performance

Steering Capability

The president of Madagascar possesses sweeping powers in comparison to other semi-presidential systems. The constitution of the Fourth Republic (2010) did little to mitigate executive strength, but it did reduce certain powers or relegate them to the policy realm, where the president maintains de facto control. In some cases, a strong presidency can be an advantage in forming a developmental state able to conduct long-term planning. However, presidential power in Madagascar is embedded in sociopolitical networks subject to electoral vicissitudes.

In terms of priority setting, 2013 was dominated by the electoral process, leaving little room for other priorities. Elections were seen as a necessary condition enabling exit from almost five years of political crisis.

The formation of a government after the 2013 elections took considerable time, as consensus had to be reached on the nomination of the prime minister.

In the first half of 2014, the general state policy has focused on strategic policies designed to create inclusive and sustainable development based on inclusive economic growth, with the aim of eradicating poverty. The highest-priority areas include strengthening governance; the rule of law and equitable justice; economic recovery; and improving access to basic social services. In practice, it is too early to judge whether these priorities can be translated into action, especially with an existing tradition of short-term vision and ministers hoping to make personal gains before being pushed out of office. Indeed, questions regarding political stability are a major challenge in maintaining and translating strategic priorities into action. Illustrating this point, the Roger Kolo government resigned on 12 January 2015 due to a lack of performance and results. A new government was installed on 25 January 2015; however, as of the time of writing, it is too early to evaluate how the government has maintained and operationalized strategic priorities.

Almost one year after the elections and the formation of a new government, a first change of government took place that will affect the implementation of strategic priorities.

The government in place as the review period closed had served only since 25 January 2015. The former government, under Prime Minister Roger Kolo, was in place less than a year (having taken office in 2014) and was not successful in setting and realizing priorities. The country faces a number of problems such as electricity cuts (JIRAMA is unable to provide electricity continuously, mainly because of poor management), plague, large amounts of garbage, unmaintained roads, illegal trafficking of all kinds (including rosewood and other natural resources), and insecurity in urban and rural areas (particularly bandits in the south). Moreover, the country did not received aid (budget support) from its international partners.

These persistent problems contributed to the pressure that resulted in the government change. However, 2014 was also year of stabilization and normalization of relations with international and regional partners. The previous year was consumed by election preparations, with the political sphere dominated by the development of consensus in organizing and accepting these elections.

New Prime Minister Ravelonarivo, a general, has indicated that the National Development Plan, the Program of Presidential Priorities, the General Policy of the State, and the main pillars of the government program will be the key documents shaping ministry activities. All ministries were requested to submit their strategic documents before 16 February 2015.

For this reason, it remains too early to judge the implementation of the new government's policies and action plans.

The year 2013 was dominated by the organization of presidential and legislative elections. The success of these elections was necessary in order to exit the political crisis, rejoin the international community and again win access international development aid. International pressure helped push the government to learn from the past and organize the elections in a transparent and credible way. This helped avoid a cyclical post-election crisis and obtain their acceptance by all stakeholders.

The price of the political crisis has been very high, and the necessity of taking action to redress the situation and tackle extreme poverty is urgent.

In this context, the elected government has shown a willingness to learn from past experiences, and has proved itself open to external recommendations and expertise. As concrete actions remain limited, it is difficult to judge how flexible the government will be in adjusting its action plans if needed.

Resource Efficiency

The government does not make efficient use of most available human, financial and organizational resources. There is a lack of transparency in recruitment and promotion. A significant number of the members of the administration were not recruited on the basis of their qualifications. This is true of the highest ranks in government, as well as of the diplomatic corps. Most ambassadors are political appointees. There are also weaknesses with regard to capacity building. Training programs for state officials lack the means to qualify them fully for their ongoing responsibilities. The fragmentation of the public service and the emergence of corporatist structures impose additional constraints and management problems. The existence of various special statuses of certain parts of the administration means that public service bodies receive broadly unequal treatment.

The General Internal Audit Directorate, which is overseen by the Ministry of Finance, rarely conducted audits during the review period. The National Assembly, which is officially tasked with overseeing public expenditure, does little to fulfill this function.

The national budget is primarily prepared by the government, and the National Assembly approves it with few modifications.

The policy of decentralization has not produced the expected results. The high concentration of civil servants in the region of Analamanga affects the state's ability to provide public services in the outlying regions. The civil service is aging, with nearly half aged 50 or above. A quarter of civil servants will retire during the 2011 – 2018 period. This will require the state to allocate considerable funds to pay pensions.

The allocation of financial resources to the provinces, regions and municipalities is not fairly organized. Most expenditure remains concentrated in the capital.

This general situation deteriorated further during the near-five-year political crisis. The newly elected institutions will have to prioritize the issue of efficiency in order to respond to donor expectations and retain eligibility for budget aid. Communal elections were postponed until 2015, but are a critical aspect of the decentralization of responsibilities and resources.

As stated by the World Bank, Madagascar is a country with many advantages, including unmatched biodiversity, great agricultural potential, mineral resources and abundant labor. With the assurance of complementarity between physical and human capital, and good governance, it could be a prosperous country. Indeed, Madagascar has shown its ability to be efficient when its resources are deployed effectively, but these periods have been punctuated by recurrent political crises. Disturbances have left the majority of the population living in a condition of extreme poverty. One of the new administration's most urgent tasks is to implement policies aimed at reversing this increasing poverty.

If this goal is to be achieved, coordinating conflicting objectives should be made a top priority, enabling the government to develop a coherent policy adequate to the numerous challenges in almost all sectors. According to the World Bank, this will require a change in governance style from the "rule of man" to the "rule of law." Rules must be clear, applied equally to all, and should be implemented through discussions with stakeholders. However, Madagascar's political system has historically been marked by a strong executive power that undermines the separation of powers and the independence of the judiciary. Political contests are structured by personal relations and influence rather than actual policy, and clientelism and favoritism are common features. Rent-seeking tendencies have emerged with increasing force, fueled by financial gains linked to the discovery of oil reserves. Bureaucratic corruption is as common as political corruption, but the latter is only rarely prosecuted. All of these practices make it difficult to develop coherent and coordinated policies.

The current government's national action plans are intended to serve as the foundation for specific ministerial plans, thus guaranteeing coherence.

According to existing data on corruption, Madagascar experienced a slight decrease in 2013 as compared to the previous year. The World Bank's 2012 Worldwide Governance Indicators reflect the detrimental effect of the political crisis on the country's governance. Madagascar scores 31.10 for its control of corruption (as compared to 54.85 in 2008).

According to the 2014 Afrobarometer report, the individuals polled perceive corruption to be widespread and worsening, particularly within political institutions. The share of individuals reporting personal experience with corruption increased slightly, from 15% of users of public administrative services in 2008 to 22% in 2013.

The various forms of corruption include petty and bureaucratic corruption, electoral and political corruption, organized crime and human trafficking (corruption and the complicity of public officials have contributed to making human trafficking possible), and corruption in the renewable-resources and extractives sectors.

Madagascar made significant efforts and advancements with regard to anti-corruption policy in the early 2000s with the passage of new legislation and institutions. However, this anti-graft struggle experienced a significant slowdown during the crisis (2009 – 2013). President resident Hery Rajaonarimampianina has declared that he wants to make the fight against corruption one of the top priorities of his term in office.

Despite some notable shortcomings, such as the absence of a freedom of information law or protection for whistleblowers, Madagascar has a rather strong anti-corruption legislative framework and largely complies with international conventions on this issue. However, the country lacks a clear policy by which to coordinate various institutions' anti-corruption efforts. In 2011, the several anti-corruption institutions decided to create an exchange and coordination platform to try to bridge this gap, but the results have not been satisfactory. Moreover, all the anti-corruption bodies are under the supervision of the executive in one way or another, which undermines their independence.

Madagascar adopted its anti-corruption law in 2004 (law No. 2004 – 030). This law criminalizes active and passive bribery, abuse of power, embezzlement of public funds, influence trading, and favoritism, among other activities. The law also details the sanctions for violating its provisions. Another law adopted in 2004 criminalizes money laundering.

The 2011 law on political parties prohibits corporate donations to political parties, but not anonymous donations. It obliges political parties to report regularly on their finances, but no specific oversight institution is identified, and there are no sanctions imposed in cases of non-compliance.

Madagascar has been party to the U.N. Convention against Corruption since 2004, and to the U.N. Convention against Transnational Organized Crime since 2005. The country ratified the African Union Convention on Preventing and Combating Corruption in 2004. The various institutions addressing the issue are as follows.

Within the judiciary:

- The Chaîne Pénale Economique Anti-Corruption (CPEAC), which deals with cases received from the Bureau Indépendant de Lutte Anti-Corruption (BIANCO) and the Service Spécialisé dans la Lutte Contre le Blanchiment des Bapitaux et le Financement du Territoire (SAMIFIN). The CPEAC is criticized for inefficiency along with the rest of the judiciary and is seen as prosecuting only the "small fish." This situation is partly explained by the fact that the service lacks sufficient resources, equipment and permanent offices.

- BIANCO is seen as effective in combating and reducing low-level corruption, but it has been largely toothless with regard to political and large-scale corruption. BIANCO does not have the mandate to open investigations on its own initiative, and ultimately lacks adequate resources to properly fulfill its mission. The members of the bureau are nominated by the president, a fact that undermines its complete independence.

- The Comité de Sauvegarde de l'Intégrité (CSI) is in charge of promoting human rights, the rule of law and the fight against corruption. Its president is nominated by the president of the republic, a fact which undermines its independence. There is only limited information regarding the actual operations and efficiency of this committee.

- SAMIFIN is in charge of the reception and analysis of reports of suspicious transactions, and transfers relevant cases to the judicial authorities. SAMIFIN faces a number of obstacles in its operation. First, the country has not adopted a national policy against money laundering, leaving the agency largely without guidance. In addition, the institution lacks adequate resources to function, and in 2014, did not even have a permanent office.

- The Direction Générale de l'Audit Interne, under the aegis of the Ministry of Finance, is expected to play a role in the fight against corruption via its oversight of the quality of public service and the use of public finances, as well as through its audit missions. The administration is considered to be understaffed, and audits are rarely conducted.

- The Supreme Court's Chamber of Accounts (Cour des Comptes de la Cour Suprême) is in charge of the control of the government's accounts, and also supervises the execution of finance laws and oversees state-owned companies and public organs. There is a lack information regarding the management of public finances.

- BTI 2016 | Madagascar 38

- Madagascar's ombudsman (Médiature de la République Malagasy) was created in 1992 as an independent public body in charge of receiving and processing citizen complaints regarding the public administration and local governments. The ombudsman is a member of the CSI.

There is no information available regarding the ombudsman's operations or efficiency.

- Madagascar's public-procurement authority (Autorité de Régulation des Marchés Publics, ARMP) was created in 2006 as an independent oversight entity to operationalize reforms to the country's public-procurement system. The body was tasked with upholding the principles of free access to public contracts, equal treatment of candidates and transparency within procurement processes. The ARMP is in charge of setting applicable norms with regard to public procurement and of their implementation. It also adopts measures to prevent and fight corruption in this domain, undertakes or commissions independent audits of the execution of public contracts, and launches investigations in cases of noncompliance. There is only limited information available concerning the operations and efficiency of the Malagasy public procurement authority, but media reports suggest that due to a lack of resources, the institution has not overseen the conduct of public-procurement operations since 2010, and that only a few public organs located in the capital city were inspected.

Consensus-Building

In general, there is a broad consensus on democracy, and there are no serious disagreements between the major political actors with regard to the desirability of a market economy. The Southern African Development Community built a consensus behind the need for free, fair and transparent elections, culminating the signing of the road map in September 2011 by 11 political parties, excepting only former President Didier Ratsiraka's party. Ratsiraka's group and some other small political parties wanted to complete the reconciliation process before the elections.

The elections took place in October and December 2013, organized with the support of the international community. The results were accepted by the main political actors. This balloting represented a major step forward, but did nothing to resolve the underlying causes and impact of the 2009 coup. Laws and institutions matter less than personal relationships and the prevailing condition of zero-sum politics. The malleability of political alliances rose again to the foreground over the nomination of the prime minister (although the 14 January 2015 nomination of the second prime minister, Jean Ravelonarivo, proved easier) and the battle over control of the National Assembly, as independent parliamentarians gravitated toward whichever political bloc seemed closest to forming a dominant coalition.

By the close of the review period, President Hery Rajaonarimampianina had secured the support of a large majority in the National Assembly.

There is a broad consensus on the value of a market-oriented economy. A first version of the market-friendly National Development Plan was discussed in the National Assembly during the review period. It was mainly accepted by the participating legislators. The forthcoming National Development Plan (prepared by the president's economic advisors) is expected to give priority to reforms that would raise the level and efficiency of pro-poor and pro-growth government spending, improve governance and strengthen institutions, increase high-return infrastructure investment, and improve the business climate.

The armed forces are not under civilian and democratic control, and played a key role throughout the crisis and the unconstitutional change of power. The military is historically weak, and has been politicized as various presidents have sought to ensure its support. President Rajaonarimampianina appointed 59 generals in December 2014 in order to guarantee their support. There are several members of the military in the new government (appointed on 25 January 2015), including the prime minister, minister of defense, the minister of economy, and the secretary general of gendarmerie. A military coup seems unlikely in the short term, and would represent a step backward for democratization.

Social, ethnic, religious, regional and political cleavages in the country are significant. Ethnic cleavages sometimes drive the dynamics of associations and initiatives, but ethnic strife is rather limited. These cleavages largely do not produce widespread violence or open, violent conflict.

The current reconciliation exercise between current and former presidents illustrates the existence of political cleavages, but has little impact on a general population that has distanced itself from politics. On 19 December 2014, President Rajaonarimampianina met all four ex-presidents under the formal auspices of the Council of Christian Churches in Madagascar (FFKM), which has been pursuing national reconciliation for years. By the end of the review period, they had met seven times. A further meeting was scheduled for March 2015, following which a regional meeting would be held with the participation of other political actors and civil-society representatives.

The regional cleavage is primarily the effect of the strong centralization of politics at the capital level and an ineffective decentralization policy. It has not been to date addressed with a coherent policy, as most important political and economic elites are based in the capital and are not broadly interested in developing the other regions. However, during the election campaign, the current president promised to tackle this issue. A first step will be the organization of communal elections in order to have elected mayors and secure an effective distribution of resources.

In the long run, only strong economic growth with an effective redistributive social component and real democratic participation at all levels of political life (village, region and state) will defuse the structural conflict in Malagasy society.

Participation of civil society in the political process is weak due to a cleavage between policymakers and the grassroots. Once institutions elected, there are few mechanisms for involving civil society in decision-making processes or agenda setting. By the same token, few civil society organizations play a watchdog role or seek to hold the government accountable. Civil society organizations are often weakly structured and internally divided, with their leaders embedded in the political process. Although some large national platforms exist, they are often weak at the grassroots level, and lack credibility and impact on decision-making processes. However, some progress was evident during the 2013 elections, during which civil society organizations were able to create platforms to educate voters and observe the elections. Moreover, the elected institutions subsequently organized some consultative meetings with civil society as a part of the law-making process. Although the past role of churches in political reconciliation processes was affected by the political crisis, the actual ongoing reconciliation process is again being facilitated by the churches.

While most reconciliation attempts organized by national and international actors failed during the transition period, the Council of Christian Churches in Madagascar (FFKM) has since December 2014 conducted a national reconciliation process between current and former presidents. The return of Marc Ravalomanana on 12 October 2014 was in the spirit of national reconciliation. After a period of detention in Antsiranana, Marc Ravalomanana was back in Antananarivo by Christmas.

Several meetings of the parties involved were organized in early 2015, after which the FFKM was slated to produce a report containing suggestions for the next step in the national reconciliation process. Although it is too early to conclude on the effectiveness of these meetings, the fact that they are taking place is crucial in the political reconciliation process.

However, these meetings have lacked transparency, and their results have not been made available to the public.

The reconciliation process represents a major step in the normalization of the political situation. It could reduce the effect of the country's prevailing winner-take-all politics, and even end the condition of exclusion and exile that has followed each crisis.

This process should be organized across the country (at the regional, district and communal levels), and should feature the participation of other political actors, civil-society representatives and traditional leaders.

International Cooperation

The government clearly aims at political and economic development through the elaboration of different strategic plans such as the National Development Plan, the Program of Presidential Priorities, the General Policy of the State and the main pillars of the government program. These key documents shape all ministry activities. All ministries were requested to submit their strategic documents before 16 February 2015.

These strategic documents are being developed through the use of external expertise and recommendations from international partners and donors. The goal is to address the alarming situation faced by Madagascar after almost five years of political crisis and international isolation. The donor community has again expressed a willingness to assist the country, and the government has responded positively. This has led to close collaboration with the international donor community (IMF, World Bank, European Union, U.N. agencies, bilateral donors), as well as to reform requirements as a condition of unlocking aid. As of the end of the review period, implementation of the joint action plans was about to start; thus, it is too early to evaluate the effectiveness and efficiency of their implementation.

During the crisis and subsequent international isolation, Madagascar was forced to seek alternatives to its usual development partners, obtaining financing and investment from new sources such as China.

Madagascar has gone through a five-year political crisis, leading to international isolation and a dramatic decline in direct cooperation. The unconstitutional change of government in 2009 undermined the international community's confidence in the county's attempts to achieve democracy and strengthen the market economy. Thus, the political crisis not only affected the democratic process (no elections were organized during the crisis period), but also the formal economy; economic activity slowed, investment stagnated, and social indicators deteriorated. A World Bank report estimates that more than 92% of Malagasy now live on less than $2 a day. The suspension of external budget support forced the government to reduce social and infrastructure spending.

Sanctions were lifted following the presidential and parliamentary elections of December 2013, which helped Madagascar regain credibility within the donor community. The IMF initiated dialogue with the government and reached agreement with the Malagasy authorities on a program that could be supported by the IMF's rapid credit facility (RCF). Other multilateral and bilateral donors followed the same path, renewing dialogue with Malagasy authorities on possible ways to support democracy and market-economic development. As an example, the European Union reestablished relations with Madagascar on 19 May 2014, and strongly indicated that it would provide support Madagascar through the 11th European Development Fund (EDF).

In the aftermath of the unconstitutional change of government in 2009, relationships between the new government and regional and international organizations collapsed. Regional organizations such as the African Union and the Southern African Development Community (SADC) were strongly involved in the mediation efforts, in monitoring the implementation of the roadmap, and the organization of the country's 2013 elections. The SADC road map signed on 17 September 2011 was invaluable in helping the country emerge from its political impasse and organize elections.

The electoral process drew considerable attention from all regional and international observers. Once the president and National Assembly were elected, Madagascar was again accepted as member of regional organizations such as the Common Market for Eastern and Southern Africa (COMESA), the SADC and the Indian Ocean Commission (IOC).

Cooperation agreements in the aviation sector, in the field of agriculture, in tourism (Vanilla Island), and in maritime safety are planned as part of the IOC. Madagascar plans to boost trade cooperation with the countries of COMESA. The country will also host the COMESA summit in 2016.

Madagascar has also cooperative agreements with countries including Mauritius (trade, agriculture, tourism) and South Africa (trade and education).

Strategic Outlook

With the 2013 elections enabling Madagascar to be reintegrated into the international community, the country faces numerous challenges. However, there seems to be a political will to develop comprehensive and coherent strategic plans to tackle these political, economic and social issues. The National Development Plan was expected to be completed in early 2015 and will provide guidance for future national and international policies.

In general, the government should make some major decisions and take significant actions to improve democracy and the economic climate. Such actions should include:

- strengthening institutions and governance at all levels;

- continuing the national reconciliation process with the participation of all relevant political, economic, military and social actors, in order to promote political stability;

- promoting the creation of political parties rooted at a national level, while regulating the participation of independent electoral candidates in order to reduce political fragmentation;

- tackling corruption and building institutional integrity (for example, by promoting the independence of BIANCO and other institutions working in the anti-corruption field);

- engaging in reforms of the security sector and judiciary (for example, by barring military officers from serving in political or civilian administrative capacities; improving maritime security; participating in peacekeeping missions; ensuring that career advancement within the military is shielded from political manipulation and in line with international best practices, and facilitating cohesion and professionalism);

- improving the national-budget development process by organizing consultation rounds with the National Assembly, the private sector and civil society;

- accelerating the decentralization process and distributing state resources more effectively;

- promoting free competition and a healthy fiscal climate, and improving infrastructure in order to stimulate growth by attracting national, regional and international investors;

- increasing fiscal maneuvering room in order to raise the level and efficiency of pro-poor/pro-growth spending while preserving the sustainability of the public debt. This must involve broadening the tax base, a comprehensive revenue-mobilization strategy, improvements in the composition and quality of public expenditure, and strengthening public financial management;

- increasing public expenditure on social protection, education and health care, especially in rural areas;

- improving the "watchdog" role of civil society, giving it the ability to oversee public actions and request accountability. This can be done through capacity building and the reinforcement of social networks; and

- improving access to information, while allowing private audiovisual media to establish national coverage.

Madagascar Government and Politics

Constitution and Institutions of Governance

The Third Republic received its first expression of popular support and legitimacy on August 19, 1992, when the constitutional framework constructed by the National Conference was approved by more than 75 percent of those voting in a popular referendum (the constitution took effect on September 12). On this date, the people overwhelmingly approved a new constitution consisting of 149 articles that provided for the separation of powers among the executive, legislative, and judicial branches of government; the creation of a multiparty political system; and the protection of individual human rights and freedom of speech.

The power of the executive branch is divided between a president who is elected by universal suffrage and a prime minister from the parliament who is nominated by his/her peers but who must be approved by the president. If the nominee for prime minister does not achieve an absolute majority of support within the parliament, the president may choose a candidate from the parliament who will seor one year. As captured in the Malagasy concept ray aman-dreny (father and mother of the nation), enshrined in Article 44 of the constitution, the president serves as the symbol of national unity. The president also is the recognized leader of foreign policy and constitutes by far the single most powerful political person within the country. All presidential decrees must be countersigned, however, and the president is bound by the constitutional reality that the prime minister is responsible for the functioning of the government.

The president is elected for a five-year period and is limited to two terms in office. In the event that no candidate wins a simple majority of the popular vote, a run-off election is held between the two leading candidates within a period of two months. The most important unwritten law regarding the executive branch revolves around the côtier/central highlands distinction. If a côtier is elected president, it is understood that a Merina will fill the position of prime minister, and vice versa. In the case of the first national elections held under the Third Republic, for example, the elected president--Zafy--who is a côtier, chose a prime minister-- Francisque Ravony--from the ranks of the Merina (although several of the Merina elite were not entirely happy with the choice because Ravony is only half Merina).

The constitution provides for a bicameral parliament composed of a Senate and a National Assembly (Assembleé Nationale). The Senate represents territorial groups and serves as the consultative chamber on social and economic issues. Two-thirds of its members are chosen by an Electoral College and the remaining one-third are chosen by the president. Envisioned elections for 1994 had not been held as of June 1994. The National Assembly consists of 138 deputies elected by universal suffrage using a proportional representation list-system. Both senators and deputies serve for four years. The June 16, 1993 elections resulted in about half the deputies elected being members of the Forces Vives. The remainder belonged to six parties of which the largest had fifteen deputies and the smallest nine deputies. The parliament as a whole operates with a variety of classic parliamentary measures, such as a vote of no confidence, that enable it to serve as a check on the power of the executive.

A new system of local governance under the constitution is known as the Decentralized Territorial Authorities (Collectivités Territoriales Décentralisées). According to the decentralization law adopted by the National Assembly in March 1994, twenty-eight regions (faritra), more than 100 departments (fileovana), and a little less than 1,000 communes (faribohitra) have been created. Certain urban communes, such as the cities of

Antananarivo, Nosy-Be, and Sainte Marie will function as departments. Envisioned as regional vehicles for popular input in which members are elected by universal suffrage, these authorities have yet to be implemented; their exact role in the policy-making process remains ill-defined, but it is contemplated that the national government will handle such areas as foreign affairs, defense, public security, justice, currency, and broad economic planning and policy, leaving economic implementation to the decentralized bodies. However, the Zafy regime is confident that, once functioning, these regional boards will take the political initiative away from the so-called federalist opposition, which has been seeking to shift power away from the central government to the regions.

A strong, independent judiciary is also enshrined in the 1992 constitution. An eleven-member Supreme Court serves as the highest arbiter of the laws of the land. Other judicial bodies include the Administrative and Financial Constitutional Court, the Appeals Courts, tribunals, and the High Court of Justice. The creation of this complex system indicates the desire of the constitutional framers for a society built upon the rule of law. Indeed, the constitution explicitly outlines the fundamental rights of individual citizens and groups (most notably freedom of speech) and guarantees the existence of an independent press free from government control or censorship.

The creation of a truly free and fair multiparty system is the centerpiece of the new constitutional order. In sharp contrast to the Ratsiraka era, when political parties could only exist under the ideological umbrella of the FNDR, democratization of the political system has led to the proliferation of political parties of all ideological stripes. In the first legislative elections held under the Third Republic in 1993, for example, more than 120 political parties fielded at least 4,000 candidates for a total of 138 legislative seats. Despite constitutional guarantees concerning the rights of citizens to form political parties without fear of government retribution, parties that call for ethnic or religious segregation or demonstrably endanger national unity are subject to being banned.

The electoral system is designed to promote and facilitate widespread popular participation. In fact, it is argued that the proportional representation list-system (including the rule of the largest remainder) for electing deputies actually encourages large numbers of candidates to take part. All resident citizens eighteen years of age or older can vote in elections, but candidates must be at least twenty-one years of age to participate. Electoral registers are usually revised during a two-month period beginning in December, and the country is divided into sixty-eight constituencies for electoral purposes. Although there was a four-month gap between the end of the first presidential elections and the first legislative elections held under the Third Republic in 1993, legislative elections are supposed to be held no less than two months after the end of presidential elections. The next presidential elections are scheduled for 1998

Madagascar The Fokonolona and Traditional Governance

Madagascar has a tradition of limited village self-rule associated with the institution of the fokonolona--a village council composed of village elders and other local notables. After having been alternately suppressed and encouraged by the French colonial authorities, authorities officially revived the fokonolona in 1962 in an attempt to involve local communities in plans for rural economic and social development. The perceived usefulness of the fokonolona derived from its traditional role of maintaining order in the village and providing social and economic assistance.

In 1973 the Ramanantsoa military regime furthered the selfrule concept by establishing self-governing bodies at the local level. Government functionaries who were formerly appointed were to be replaced by elected officials. Yet it was not until 1975, under the leadership of Ratsiraka, that the fokonolona was given constitutional recognition as the "decentralized collective of the state" responsible for economic, social, cultural, and municipal development at the local level. Despite his best intentions, during Ratsiraka's rule the fokonolona was still far from an idealized self-governing institution. Its governing bodies were dominated, as in the past, by conservative elders, and participation by youth was either minimal or not encouraged by elders. Under the Zafy regime the fokonolona will continue to offer policy guidance at the local level, but it has been superseded by the Decentralized Territorial Collectives.

The fokonolona often is characterized as one of the most characteristic Malagasy social institutions. It is, in fact, not a "pan-Malagasy" cultural element but an institution that evolved among the Merina and was implanted in other parts of the country by both the Merina and the French. Even among the neighboring Betsileo, it is considered something of a foreign implantation. Nonetheless, the fokonolona offers aid to members in need (such as when a child is born or a funeral is held), undertakes village projects (such as the repair of rice fields or village buildings after a cyclone), coordinates mutual aid at planting and harvest time, and occasionally chastises--or ostracizes--those considered wrongdoers.

The fokonolona ties individuals together in a network of mutual obligations. Its meetings bring together in a cooperative setting people of different kinship groups within a village, and the common use of fictive kinship terms promotes the creation of an atmosphere of amity and solidarity (fihavanana), necessary for sincere cooperation. The fokonolona, however, traditionally has not been a democratic institution despite its town-meeting character, because its meetings tend to be dominated by influential local notables. Local political power remains a function of age and membership in a high-status kinship group; in some cases, the descendants of slaves (andevo) attend fokonolona meetings, but their influence is marginal.

At fokonolona meetings, it is possible to see one of Madagascar's most striking cultural expressions, the kabary (discourse), a lengthy speech in which a speaker uses flowery and poetic language to make a critical point in a most indirect fashion. The people will listen silently from beginning to end. Those who disagree will not express their opinion but will counter with a speech that at first seems to support the first speaker but that actually contains a hidden counterproposal. Speakers may express their views by telling jokes. If people laugh or if they simply act according to the second speaker's proposal, the first has lost. Rarely if ever does an open confrontation between speakers occur.

Madagascar Foreign Relations

Close Franco-Malagasy ties formed the cornerstone of Madagascar's foreign policy in the early independence years, as witnessed by the signing of fourteen agreements and conventions with France. An Economic and Financial Cooperation Agreement signed in June 1960 specified and regulated Madagascar's status as a member of the Franc Zone. Other economic agreements ensured the sanctity of existing French economic interests and, therefore, continued strong levels of French influence over Madagascar's economy. The Malagasy role was largely limited to the impact of decision makers in the upper echelons of government and input at the grass-roots level by small-scale farmers producing for subsistence or export. Other sectors by and large remained the domain of French trading conglomerates, large-scale agriculturalists, or Chinese and Indian middlepersons.

In the realm of security, defense agreements underscored France's willingness to provide strategic protection for Madagascar. France was allowed access to military bases and installations in Madagascar. These included the natural harbor of Antsiranana at the northern end of the island and the Ivato airfield near Antananarivo. France also enjoyed complete freedom of movement in the island's airspaces and coastal waters. In return for these benefits, France provided military aid, technical assistance, and training for Malagasy security forces.

French influence was equally strong in the cultural realm. The country's intellectual elite was French-speaking, and many prominent Malagasy studied in French lycées and acquired degrees from French universities. Newspapers and periodicals published in French as well as Malagasy circulated in Antananarivo and other major cities. French was the language of instruction for higher education, and many teachers were French. At secondary and higher levels, the curriculum was modeled closely on that of France.

The strengthening of ties with France was complemented by a desire to enhance links with other Western countries, including Britain, Italy, Switzerland, the Federal Republic of Germany (West Germany), and most notably the United States. In October 1963, the Tsiranana regime consented to the construction of a National Aeronautics and Space Administration (NASA) satellite tracking station near the old airport outside the capital. In return, the United States initiated a modest foreign assistance program that guaranteed private investment in the island's economy and made available a number of fellowships to students from Madagascar. Madagascar also established diplomatic links with other newly emerging nations, particularly former French colonies in Africa, and strengthened relationships with Asian countries, most notably Japan, India, and Indonesia.

A significant shift occurred in Madagascar's foreign policy after the downfall of the Tsiranana regime in 1972. In a series of diplomatic moves that three years later were embraced by the Ratsiraka regime as the cornerstones of the Second Republic, the Ramanantsoa regime pronounced Madagascar's commitment to nonalignment, anti-imperialism, anticolonialism, and antiracism in international affairs. In the context of the privileged Franco-Malagasy relationship, these themes translated into harsh rhetoric concerning the necessity of revoking the "slavery agreements" of the Tsiranana regime, followed by the uncompensated nationalization of all French banks and insurance firms in June 1975, contributing to the dramatic cooling of diplomatic relations. Moreover, in June 1976, the Ratsiraka regime laid claim to small, rocky, French-held islands around Madagascar, including the Glorieuses (claimed concurrently by Comoros), Juan de Nova, Europa, Bassas da India, and Tromelin (also claimed by Mauritius). Originally administered as part of French-ruled Madagascar, these possessions were split off just prior to independence in 1960 and include some minor military facilities.

Diplomatic links also soured with other Western powers, such as Britain, which closed its embassy in 1975. In the case of the United States, the immediate cause of strained ties was the Ratsiraka regime's decision to close the NASA tracking station.

Another source of friction was the frequent verbal assaults by the Ratsiraka regime against the United States military presence at Diego Garcia Island. The Malagasy position was that, in accordance with a UN resolution passed in 1971, the Indian Ocean should be a demilitarized, nuclear-free zone of peace. Nonetheless, trade relations remained essentially unaffected, and diplomatic relations continued, albeit at the reduced level of chargés d'affaires.

The most dramatic development was the strengthening of ties with Eastern Europe and with other communist regimes. After establishing diplomatic links with the Soviet Union in October 1972--followed one month later by the establishment of ties with China and the Democratic People's Republic of Korea (North Korea)--ties were enhanced in the economic, cultural, and politico-military realms. Soviet development assistance was directed toward the fields of agriculture, medicine, science, and technology, and scholarships were provided to at least 2,000 Malagasy students to study in the Soviet Union. A new Malagasy-Soviet Intergovernmental Commission on Economic and Technical Cooperation and Trade facilitated these links. The Soviet Union was particularly interested in promoting security ties with the Ratsiraka regime. In addition to providing military advisers and technical advice, the former Soviet Union became the primary source of military equipment for the Malagasy

Armed Forces, including providing access to MiG-21 Fishbed jet fighters, and aided in the construction of a series of sealane intercept stations along Madagascar's west coast astride the Mozambique Channel. These stations were eventually dismantled in 1983 after protests by the West.

Relationships with other communist countries developed in a variety of fields. Whereas Cuba provided technical assistance within the educational realm, China funded the construction of roads between Moramanga and Toamasina, and built a new sugar factory near Morondava. The Ratsiraka regime was especially impressed by North Korean leader Kim Il Sung and his ideology of national self-reliance known as juche (or chuch'e), hosting an international conference on this topic in Antananarivo in 1976. North Korean assistance was fairly extensive in the fields of agriculture and irrigation. The North Koreans were most noted, however, for their training of Ratsiraka's presidential security unit and the construction of a presidential bunker at Iavohola.

New directions in foreign policy were equally pronounced in Madagascar's relationships with other developing countries and its positions in a variety of international forums. In addition to breaking ties with Israel and South Africa, the Ramanantsoa/Ratsiraka regimes strengthened links with Libya, the Palestine Liberation Organization, and liberation movements in southern Africa and the Western Sahara. Madagascar also joined the Nonaligned Movement, became more active in the Organization of African Unity (OAU), and took positions in the UN that favored the communist states, including abstaining on a resolution that denounced the Soviet Union's invasion of Afghanistan in 1979 and supporting Vietnam's invasion of Cambodia in 1978. In conjunction with his Cuban and Soviet allies, Ratsiraka even tried to broker an end to rising tensions between Marxist Ethiopia and Marxist Somalia just prior to the outbreak of the Ogaden War in 1977-78.

Despite some alarmist projections that the communist countries would replace the West and turn Madagascar into a Soviet satellite, the changes in Madagascar's foreign policies represented a short-term shift rather than a true break with the past. The Ratsiraka regime had gained little in the form of economic assistance from its friendly relations with the Soviet Union and other communist countries--aid from these sources constituted less than 1 percent of all bilateral assistance from 1977 to 1980--and was confronted with the harsh realities of economic decline. As a result, an increasingly pragmatic Ratsiraka sought to reaffirm and strengthen Madagascar's foreign policy relationships with the West. Indeed, relations with the West appeared to be on the upswing at the beginning of the

1980s, whereas those with the communist countries were more or less static--despite the similarity of views on a wide range of international issues routinely reaffirmed by the spokespersons of Madagascar and of communist countries. As was the case with other self-proclaimed Marxist regimes during the 1970s and the 1980s, Ratsiraka pursued politico-military links with the Soviet Union while seeking to maintain economic ties with the West.

Diplomatic overtures to France served as the logical starting point for achieving a balance in Madagascar's foreign policy relationships. As early as 1977, Ratsiraka provided assurances concerning compensation for French firms nationalized during the mid-1970s in order to foster greater official and private investment in Madagascar. France responded positively, as demonstrated by the tremendous increase in foreign assistance from US$38.4 million in 1979 to US$96.4 million in 1982. Indeed, as of the early 1980s, France remained Madagascar's most important foreign policy partner. It was the principal source of foreign assistance and the most valuable trading partner. The dispute over French control of neighboring islands, although unresolved, had little if any ill effect on Franco-Malagasy relations, mainly because the Ratsiraka regime no longer publicly pressed this issue in international forums. (The motion asking France to cede the islands had been adopted by the UN

General Assembly by a ninety-seven to seven vote in 1979 with thirty-six abstentions.)

The diversification of ties, thereby avoiding dependence on any single power, served as another cornerstone of Madagascar's foreign policy initiatives during the 1980s. Relations were fully restored with Washington in November 1980 when United States Ambassador Fernando E. Rondon assumed his post for the first time since his predecessor had been recalled during the summer of 1975. Receiving the new envoy, Ratsiraka expressed the hope that "fruitful, loyal, and lasting cooperation" would develop between the two countries and that there would be "no further misunderstandings" as a result of differing opinions on international issues. Other major events included the reopening of the British embassy in 1979, Ratsiraka's visits with President Ronald Reagan in Washington in 1982 and 1983, the opening of a World Bank office in Antananarivo in 1983, and the strengthening of links with other industrialized countries, most notably Japan.

The levels of foreign assistance provided by the West demonstrate the success of Ratsiraka's diplomatic initiatives. Bilateral aid from the West constituted only US$36.3 million one year after Ratsiraka had taken power in 1975. Four years after the beginning of the foreign policy changes initiated by the

Ramantsoa regime, this amount increased to US$168.1 million in 1982, to US$217.6 million in 1988, and to US$365.5 million in 1991. Similarly, multilateral assistance from Western financial institutions, such as the IMF and the European Common Market (European Union), increased from US$34.1 million in 1976 to US$80.6 million in 1982, to US$108.9 million in 1988, and to US$191.4 million in 1991.

Equally important, Ratsiraka's policies led to a diversification of Madagascar's sources of foreign assistance. Although France in 1991 still provided approximately 43 percent (US$157.0 million) of Madagascar's bilateral foreign assistance, in 1988 it had provided approximately 50 percent (US$108.5 million). The amount marked a significant decline from almost total dependence in 1970 when nearly 90 percent of all Western assistance was provided by France. Noteworthy, however, was France's provision of US$655.4 million of the total US$1,334.5 million multilateral aid that Madagascar received between 1985 and 1990. In addition, France gave Madagascar loan assistance for such projects as telecommunications, transportation, and banking, and canceled US$715 million in debts that the Madagascar government owed France. In 1993 Madagascar received about US$167 million in aid from France compared with about US$152 million in aid received from France in 1992. Whereas the United States provided US$71.0 million in multilateral aid in 1991, Japan and Germany extended US$56.8 million and US$30.3 million respectively.

United States direct development aid has become increasingly important for Madagascar and has risen from about US$10 million in 1990 to US$13.5 million in 1991 (US$28 million were authorized but could not be used because of strikes and the disrupted political and economic situation), US$40 million in 1992, and US$40.6 million in 1993. Of the 1993 total, US$20.4 million was earmarked for environmental protection and US$10 million for the private sector.

The growing partnership with the West was cemented by dramatic changes in the international system and in Madagascar's domestic political system. The fall of the Berlin Wall in 1989 signaled the beginning of a process eventually leading to the downfall of communist regimes and trading partners in Eastern Europe, the fragmentation of the Soviet Union, and the increasing international isolation of North Korea and Cuba as pariah regimes. Furthermore, this international trend facilitated the rise of popular pressures for a multiparty democracy in Madagascar, eventually leading to the downfall of Ratsiraka's Second Republic and its replacement in 1993 with a democratically inspired Third Republic under the leadership of Zafy.

The cornerstone of Madagascar's foreign policy in the post- Cold War era is the continued diversification of ties, with an emphasis on promoting economic exchanges. In addition to establishing formal diplomatic ties with the Republic of Korea (South Korea) in May 1993, negotiations were initiated to restore diplomatic links with Israel and South Africa. In each of these cases, diplomatic links are perceived as the precursor to lucrative trading agreements. For example, one month after establishing diplomatic ties with South Korea, Madagascar hosted a South Korean trade mission that included representatives of six major South Korean companies: Daewoo, Dong Yong Electronics, Hyundai, Kolon, Peace Industries, and Samsung. As underscored by Prime Minister Ravony, one of the most critical challenges facing Madagascar is the restructuring of its embassies and foreign policy to "objectives of economic redeployment" in the post-Cold War era. Of particular interest to Madagascar, in view of their proximity and commercial potential, are relations and trade with India, Mauritius, Australia, and South Africa.

The benefits associated with changes in the international environment have an impact on Madagascar's domestic political system. Similar to other newly installed African democracies at the beginning of the 1990s, the Zafy regime confronts the challenge of consolidating still-fragile democratic practices and governing institutions in a significantly changed international environment. Although such potential benefits associated with the end of the Cold War as a renewed focus on economic as opposed to military investments have been heralded by Western observers, the leaders of African countries, including Madagascar, rightfully wonder if their countries will be further marginalized as former benefactors either turn inward or toward more lucrative economic markets in Asia and Latin America. Equally important, the Zafy regime faces balancing rising public demands to receive immediately the fruits of democratization with the harsh reality of the political constraints of a democratic system. Indeed, democratization has not proved to be a quick panacea to resolving such issues as the necessity of overhauling and privatizing largely inert and bloated state-operated economic enterprises, and has even led to the emergence of new problems, most notably federalist demands for greater regional autonomy. Nonetheless, Madagascar's political elite clearly seems committed to the continued reform and strengthening of multiparty democracy, as well as the expansion of the country's role as a leader in both regional and international forums.

Madagascar's political rights Measure

Madagascar's political rights rating improved from 4 to 3 due to competitive local elections in July and greater transparency in the drafting of legislation.

Overview

Madagascar continued its progress toward democratic consolidation in 2015. Competitive elections for local government positions in July and the Senate in December completed the return to democratic government after Andry Rajoelina's 2009 military-backed coup. The National Assembly voted to impeach President Hery Rajaonarimampianina in May 2015, citing his failure to uphold the constitution, but a court ruling struck down the attempt.

Madagascar launched the "Fahalemana 2015" operation in August 2015 to combat widespread insecurity in the south from organized groups of cattle thieves. The state has only nominal control over the south of the country, where local security forces are often viewed to be complacent or cooperative with armed groups. Eight members of the army were killed in an ambush in August 2015. Human rights groups have highlighted security forces' abuses of citizens, including summary executions.

International funding has resumed since the 2009 coup and ensuing political crisis, but the fall in global commodities prices has undercut the mining sector, which serves as the main source of foreign investment. Large demonstrations took place in the coastal city of Toamasina in December 2014 and January 2015 over persistent outages from the power company, Jirama, and citizen perceptions of widespread corruption in the energy sector.

Political Rights and Civil Liberties:
Political Rights: 24 / 40 (+2)
A. Electoral Process: 9 / 12

The president and the lower house of parliament, the National Assembly, are directly elected to five-year terms. The 151 seats in the National Assembly are filled through a mix of party-list voting in multimember constituencies and majoritarian contests in single-member districts. The National Assembly nominates the prime minister and the president appoints the nominee. While the 2010 constitution calls for the establishment of a Senate, no members were chosen until December 2015. The president appoints one-third of the 33-member Senate while the remaining two-thirds are indirectly elected from each of the 22 districts of Madagascar. President Rajaonarimampianina's party, Hery Vaovao Madagasikara (HVM), won 65 percent of the vote. The formation of the Senate will mark the first time that the full executive and legislative bodies of Madagascar will fully function since Rajoelina ousted then-President Ravalomanana in a 2009 military coup.

Elections for the National Assembly took place in 2013 alongside the country's presidential elections. The parliamentary elections were deemed free and fair by international observers, though several hundred thousand people were left off the voter rolls during the election's first round. The With Andry Rajoelina (MAPAR) party won 49 of 151 parliamentary seats, the Ravalomanana Movement took 20, the Vondrona Politika Miara-Dia–Malagasy Miara-Miainga (VPM-MMM) party won 13, and various other parties and independent candidates took the remainder. For the presidency, Rajaonarimampianina—a former finance minister backed by Rajoelina—was elected with 54 percent of the vote. After taking office, Rajaonarimampianina broke from Rajoelina's influence.

In January 2015, opposition dissatisfaction led to the resignation of the prime minister. Continued dissatisfaction among opposition factions led to the new prime minister narrowly escaping a no-confidence vote in July. Meanwhile, the required two-thirds of the National Assembly voted in May 2015 to impeach President Rajaonarimampianina, citing his deliberate mixing of religion and politics and his failure to uphold the constitution. The High Constitutional Court ruled against the National Assembly's decision in June, calling the attempt unfounded. Rajoelina and members of his party, MAPAR, continued to call for the president to step down and for early elections to be held.

In July 2015 regional and municipal elections, Rajaonarimampianina's HVM won more than half the races. Though the electoral process was free and fair, there were accusations of inaccurate voter rolls and use of state resources for campaigning. Confusion over the electoral rules prior to the municipal elections advantaged state campaigns over smaller parties. The mandate of the transitional electoral management body ended after the municipal elections, and the government established a new independent body.

Political Pluralism and Participation: 10 / 16 (+1)

Despite restrictions on opposition political activity during the transitional period under Rajoelina, political parties were generally able to operate ahead of the national elections in 2013, when 33 candidates ran for president. Rajaonarimampianina established his own party leading up to the presidential elections. In 2015 local elections, multiple opposition parties competed, many of which have advanced policies and platforms against the government.

The return of former president Marc Ravalomanana from exile in 2014, and his release from house arrest in May 2015, destabilized parliamentary alliances as he worked to reestablish his nascent political party structure. Ravalomanana was sentenced in 2010 in absentia to life in prison with hard labor for allegedly ordering the killing of at least 30 opposition protesters in 2009. He has not received amnesty for the conviction. In a test of his party's return to politics, Ravalomanana's wife, Lalao, won the mayoralty in Antananarivo in 2015.

Functioning of Government: 5 / 12 (+1)

Elected officials are susceptible to outside influence; the large number of independent candidates in the National Assembly, as well as Rajaonarimampianina's constantly shifting coalition, have facilitated opportunities for vote buying among legislators.

Though Rajaonarimampianina has committed to reducing corruption, the independent anticorruption bureau released a report in September 2015 stating that corrupt activity has stayed level or worsened since the president took office. Funding for the bureau decreased for 2015. Madagascar was ranked 123 out of 168 countries and territories surveyed in Transparency International's 2015 Corruption Perceptions Index.

Despite a 2010 decree that prohibited the logging, transport, trading, and export of precious woods, the illegal trade continues. In 2014, the Extractive Industries Transparency Initiative (EITI) lifted its three-year suspension of Madagascar, citing the commitments of the newly elected government to EITI standards. Illegally harvested rosewood and other precious timbers continue to be smuggled offshore with low levels of government intervention and occasional official complicity in the practice. Finance budgets are open to the public and introduced in parliament. The government has added civil society positions to lawmaking panels.

Civil Liberties: 30 / 60 (+2)
Freedom of Expression and Belief: 10 / 16 (+1)

The constitution provides for freedoms of speech and of the press. While Rajoelina's transitional government routinely ignored press freedom, the current government has demonstrated greater respect for media freedom and freedom of expression. Government censorship and intimidation of journalists continue, though at lower levels. There are a variety of newspaper, radio, and television outlets available to citizens, though political leaders own or operate several of the papers as a means to promote their party and personal interests. The state-run radio and television stations favor the government. The government occasionally interferes with the media, including in 2015 radio and television stations owned by Ravalomanana and Rajoelina. In August 2015, unknown assailants ransacked and destroyed a MAPAR-backed television station in the city of Fianarantsoa following its criticism of municipal election results. However, violence against journalists has generally decreased. A 2014 cybercrime law punishes online defamation of state officials with up to five years' imprisonment.

The Malagasy people have traditionally enjoyed religious freedom. In April 2015, the government relaxed limitations on a Protestant church closely associated with Ravalomanana, which was subject to frequent government intervention during the transition period. Academic freedom is generally respected.

Associational and Organizational Rights: 8 / 12

Rajaonarimampiana's administration has eased the freedom of assembly restrictions imposed after the 2009 coup. Repression of political gatherings has generally declined in the past two years and political rallies in the lead-up to the 2015 elections were rarely prevented. Nevertheless, political demonstrators are still occasionally subject to violence from security forces or restrictions on assembly.

Freedom of association is generally respected, and hundreds of nongovernmental organizations, including human rights groups, are active. Workers have the right to join unions, engage in collective bargaining, and strike. However, more than 80 percent of workers are engaged in agriculture, fishing, and forestry at a subsistence level and therefore have no access to unions.

Rule of Law: 6 / 16

The judiciary remains susceptible to corruption and executive influence. In 2014, Rajaonarimampianina appointed a new president and three additional new members to the High Constitutional Court (HCC). Although legal, the new appointments were in the president's interests and raised concerns about the separation of powers. In June 2015, the HCC ruled against the National Assembly's vote to impeach the president. Judges evaluating the hundreds of complaints submitted over the 2015 electoral process were largely seen to be impartial, though they reportedly received a number of unspecified threats. The executive continues to exert pressure on judges through reassigning magistrates to different locations.

A lack of training, resources, and personnel hampers judicial effectiveness, and case backlogs are lengthy. More than half of the people held in the country's prisons are pretrial detainees, and prisoners suffer from harsh and sometimes life-threatening conditions due to overcrowding and substandard hygiene and health care. Parliament unanimously voted to abolish the death penalty in 2014. Customary-law courts in rural areas continue to lack due process guarantees and regularly issue summary and severe punishments.

The army and security forces demonstrated neutrality during the 2015 impeachment attempt and the municipal elections, though loyalty in the security forces is historically fractured between different political movements. The police and military are unable to assert authority over the entirety of Madagascar. In addition, cattle thieves, known as dahalo, exist in portions of the south and often collude with security officials. In August 2015, the government launched a large security operation against the dahalos, leading to reports of military involvement in a number of civilian deaths and summary executions of suspected thieves.

A political cleavage has traditionally existed between the coastal côtier and the highland Merina peoples, of continental African and Southeast Asian origins, respectively. Due to past military conquest and longstanding political dominance, the Merina tend to have higher status than the côtier. Ethnicity, caste, and regional solidarity often lead to discrimination. Same-sex sexual relations are not criminalized, but LGBT (lesbian, gay, bisexual, and transgender) people still face discrimination from some segments of the state and society.

Personal Autonomy and Individual Rights: 8 / 16 (+1)

Despite decentralized village patrols and the escalation of government operations, dahalo groups hamper the free movement of citizens in certain regions. Security patrols cease operations after dark. Dahalo raids have led to an uptick in internally displaced people.

Madagascar's legal structure provides protections for private property rights, and secured interests in property are recognized though not entirely enforced. The vast majority of farmers do not hold the official rights to their land. Foreigners are prohibited from owning land. Citizens, companies, and foreign entities are able to buy and sell property, though corruption impedes proper functioning of the system.

The proportion of women in parliament increased from 17.5 percent to 20.5 percent after the 2013 elections. Women still face societal discrimination and enjoy fewer opportunities than men for higher education and employment. Though women are legally allowed to own land, when a couple applies for certification it will appear, at least 80 percent of the time, in only the man's name. According to the U.S. State Department's 2015

Trafficking in Persons Report, Madagascar has improved its efforts to reduce trafficking of men, women, and children into forced labor and sex work at home and abroad. The government created a human trafficking bureau in March 2015 and began a nationwide awareness campaign in July.

Women's Access to Political Leadership in Madagascar: The Value of History and Social Political Activism

Intellectual

Globally, wide gaps exist between men's and women's participation in leadership roles. This paper explores women's access to leadership in Madagascar through an examination of women's participation in politics and government. Research across the literature found three major reasons for women's political participation: gender quotas, kinship and societal upheaval. However, upon examining Madagascar, women's participation in leadership involves factors, which were not fully explored in this literature. The historical legacy of Madagascar and women's social and political activism were the principal factors in women's participation in leadership. The findings might have implications in explaining women's access to leadership roles.

Women's Access to Leadership in Madagascar

While women have admittedly gained more representation in the political arena, there are still major discrepancies between female political participation and that of their male counterparts (Brown & Diekman, 2013). This is the case with regard to politics as well as business and other aspects of daily life. As of January 2014, there are only nine heads of state who are women and fourteen women who are heads of government. Women also only form 21.8% of national parliamentarians and 17% of government ministers are women (United Nations Women, 2014). In all of the history of the United States, only 44 women have served in the Senate, and 32 have ever been elected as governors (Center for American Women and Politics, 2014). The active participation of women in leadership is an integral part of development, as women constitute half of the world's population (World Bank, 2013). Non-governmental organizations and civil society organizations such as the United Nations (United Nations Women, 1979) advocate for a more equitable participation of women in leadership positions and more participation of women in decision-making in general.

Currently in Madagascar, a country with a population of 22.92 million people (World Bank, 2013), women form 23% of the national parliament. Based on this figure, Madagascar ranks 73rd in the world for women in parliament (The International

Parliamentary Union, 2014). Current advocacy initiatives attempt to bolster women's participation in politics and other areas of leadership through women's education and empowerment among other measures (Women's Leadership and Political Participation, 2015). However, in order to know what methods are best for promoting women's leadership, it is necessary to examine why women participate in leadership roles, and how they have access to those roles. The question for Madagascar therefore, and the question that this research seeks to address is; what accounts for women's leadership roles in politics and government in Madagascar?

In order to develop policies and programs that foment women's participation in politics and societal leadership, it is necessary to first know what contributes to women's participation and by extension, what barriers exist to prevent women from gaining access to leadership. This research will explore the case in Madagascar because, as the literature will show, there is a lack of research around the specific factors that contribute to women's leadership in politics in that country. This research may also be relevant to other countries besides Madagascar and the findings may be useful in informing policy and programs that seek to increase women's participation in leadership in general.

Literature Review

Various theories have been explored as to how women gain political leadership positions, and what barriers they face to their participation in politics. Jalalzai and Krook (2010) outline differences between women's attainment of national leadership positions, and leadership positions in national parliaments. One of the reasons they cite is kinship—women whose husbands or fathers had been in politics found a road already paved for their own entrance into the political arena. This is especially the case historically in terms of national leadership. Jalalzai and Krook (2010) provide examples such as Indira Gandhi of India and Michelle Bachelet of Chile to make this point.

The electoral system also plays an important role in women's leadership both at the national and parliamentary levels. Nationally, some political systems have both a prime ministerial and a presidential office. Women may get elected to the office that has less power in decision making and influence in the country, in essence being just figure-heads (Jalalzai and Krook, 2010). On the parliamentary level, the type of electoral system plays a role in women's attainment of leadership positions. Whether the system is one of proportional representation or majority determines women's participation (Jalalzai and Krook, 2010). If an electoral system includes enforced quotas that address women's participation in politics, then this increases women's political participation (Krook, 2013). However, there can be bias in the implementation of these quotas. As Ryan, Haslam, and Kulich (2010) note, based on their study of the 2005 United Kingdom general elections, women are often times appointed to contest seats that they have little chance of winning. While Ryan, Haslam and Kulich admit that there might be many factors attributing to this, the fact remains that it has an effect on women's attainment of leadership positions.

There is also a distinction made between whether a female is elected to a position or appointed. According to Jalalzai and Krook (2010), some systems are dual systems where both a president and a prime minister form the head of the government. In these systems, women may sometimes be appointed to the position of less power, and subject to dismissal at the whim of the president. So while they are in theory in important positions of leadership, their power is in fact

limited. The literature also seems to posit that women in appointed positions often do not get elected after the end of their term (Jalalzai and Krook, 2010; Ryan, Haslam, & Kulich, 2010). For instance, where a female is a vice president and the president becomes unable to continue in his office, the female then becomes the president (Jalalzai and Krook, 2010). While this is a possible route to leadership for these female leaders, they are often not re-elected to office (Jalalzai and Krook, 2010).

Another cited reason for women's political participation is instability (Jalalzai and Krook, 2010; Brown and Diekman, 2013; Krook, 2013; Ryan, Haslam, and Kulich, 2010). Jalalzai and Krook (2010) posit women's traditional roles as the reason for their elections during unstable times. But they also argue that in turbulent times, a candidate's qualities as a leader are more important than their gender, and this is the reason women are easily elected during those times. This idea is reinforced by Ryan, Haslam, and Kulich (2010), who claim that traditional women's traits are more useful in times of crisis. According to Brown and Diekeman's (2013) System Justification Theory, political instability leads to social change; if people are satisfied with the current system, they are less likely to support a non-traditional leader. When they are unsatisfied, they are more likely to support women and minorities in leadership roles. Krook (2013) attributes low female political participation in Botswana to the country's decades of political and social stability, arguing that stability does not foster change.

Another factor that affects women's access to leadership is the impact of a country's history on the current situation of women in that country. Case studies of Rwanda (Herndon and Randell, 2013) and Malawi (Tiessen, 2008) make mention of the historical legacy of these countries and the effects these legacies have on women in the present. In the case of pre-colonial

Rwanda, women held a high status because of their child-bearing abilities; however, it is arguable whether this has any bearing on Rwandan women's current high rates of political participation. According to Herndon and Randell (2013), the main reason for Rwanda's current high rate of female participation in politics— 63.8% women parliamentarians in the lower house (United Nations Women 2014) —is because of the social upheaval caused by the Rwandan genocide. Herndon and Randell's (2013) study is a case for the theory of instability discussed earlier (Jalalzai and Krook, 2010; Brown and Diekman, 2013; Krook, 2013; Ryan, Haslam, and Kulich, 2010).

In the case of Malawi, Tiessen (2008) argues that the history of women's subjugation in the country now contributes to women's low participation rates in politics and access to leadership roles. However, Tiessen's (2008) argument is more tied to culture as well, not just history. This same case may be made for Rwanda— culture and historical legacy in both Rwanda and Malawi have some effect on women's access to leadership in the present day. Jalalzai and Krook (2010) argue that leadership roles of women in politics are affected by religion, culture, and ideology (Jalalzai and Krook 2010). In the case of Madagascar, this present research seeks to explore a different aspect of history that may now have an influence on women's political leadership. Instead of viewing history through a cultural lens of perceptions of women and their roles, this paper instead focuses on women in leadership in the history of Madagascar.

Does a historical legacy of women in political leadership affect women's access to leadership roles? Perkins, Phillips and Pearce (2013) argue that the presence of women in leadership serves as a source of inspiration for other women to become leaders. Their theory refers to real-time situations, and this research also seeks to explore how past female political leaders affect women's access to leadership in the present.

Proposition

While the electoral system, kinship ties, quotas, culture, religion and ideology all have an impact on women's accessibility to leadership, we propose that women have greater access to leadership roles in a country where there is a historical legacy of women in leadership positions, as well as active participation of women in the areas of advocacy and social and political activism. Madagascar is a country with a history of women in political leadership as monarchs who had absolute power. It is also a country where currently, women are involved in activism, whether it is social, political, or advocacy. Therefore, these factors may have as important an impact on women's access to political leadership as the other factors so far listed in the existing literature.

Research Methodology

The overall approach to research in this study was the stylized approach. This method was used because the research undertaken was basic research, and it contributes more to the theory and the body of knowledge of the topic of women in leadership than it contributes to immediate solutions to women's participation as in the project-based cycle (Sumner & Tribe, 2008).

In conducting this research, primarily qualitative methods were utilized; however, quantitative data was also used to a lesser degree. Therefore, the method was a mixed method. The data collection focused on: (1) The history of Madagascar as it relates to female political leaders, and what effect, if any, this history has on current women's access to leadership in the country and; (2) Women's activism in Madagascar and whether this activism leads to greater access to women's leadership in politics and government.

In the analysis, reports of non-governmental organizations that work in Madagascar which include the Electoral Institute for Sustainable Democracy in Africa, the Norwegian Agency for Development Cooperation and the Southern African Development Community were used to understand the current state of gender and politics in Madagascar. Reports of the United Nations and the World Bank were also used in this analysis.

In addition, archival research was carried out on historical records and accounts of Madagascar. Content analysis was also necessary to determine what methods are used currently to foment women's political participation in the country.

Findings/Analysis

Historical Legacy

Before the colonization of Madagascar by the French in 1896, the island of Madagascar had been partially under the control of the Merina Kingdom (Kent, 1962; Ellis, 2003). According to Ellis (2003), the Merina only ever controlled two-thirds of the island; however, the French, British and the United States had acknowledged the rulers of the Merina kingdom as the rulers of Madagascar. Before the period of unification, the island had been divided into various tribes which had their autonomous leaders and governmental structures. Among the Merina monarchs, women figured prominently, often holding absolute power over the government of the kingdom. As a matter of fact, Queen Rafohy was the Merina monarch who initially began the unification of tribes under one ruler (Kent, 1962; Raharijaona et Susan Kus, 2010). She began this unification during the first half of the sixteenth century, and it continued under various monarchs until 1787 when Andrianampoinimerina managed to unify the entire central plateau of Madagascar. Kent (1962) mentions that during this time period, succession to the throne was treacherous because it involved subterfuge, assassination, and exile, but even from then, women held absolute power as monarchs in Madagascar.

The unification of the island continued under Radama I who was succeeded by Queen Ranavalona I in 1828 (Kent, 1962; Ellis, 2003). Queen Ranavalona sought to extend Merina supremacy throughout the entire island of Madagascar. According to Kent's (1962) historical account, Ranavalona used her power to undo all the policies and practices of her predecessor Radama I, especially as regards foreign policy. King Radama had become influenced by European values, especially those perpetuated by Christian missionaries who had come to the island (Rich, 2004; Ellis, 2003). As a result, according to Rich (2004), he had sought to change many aspects of the Malagasy culture to fit the European concept of what constitutes a civilized society. One of these changes included the dominance of males in leadership in direct contrast to Malagasy tradition which had also allowed for female leadership (Rich, 2004). Ranavalona I sought to restrict foreign entrance and interference into the internal affairs Madagascar and shunned western influences, including Christianity. Kent and Raharijaona and Susan Kus, (1962; 2010) make no mention of Ranavalona I being a figurehead ruler controlled by others. She herself held the reins of power and had absolute sway over the affairs of the kingdom.

Queen Ranavalona represents the absolute political power that women held in Madagascar. She was a monarch who held absolute power over her subjects (Chernock, 2013). The contrast between this notion of an absolute female monarch and western notions of women as monarchs is evident in Ranavalona I's interaction with her British counterparts. Her grip on power was an issue for the British political leaders who had a different concept of the role of women in politics and government. Ranavalona I ruled simultaneously with Queen Victoria of Britain, and British politicians and leaders viewed Ranavalona I as having too much power simply because she was a woman (Chernock, 2013). Chernock (2013) mentions that Ranavalona herself was confused by the British political system because she was always sent official addresses from men, but not from Queen Victoria, and she stated that she would respond to no one except the ruler of the country, and as the monarch of Madagascar herself, she believed the only one who should have been able to address her was Queen Victoria.

In historical accounts, Ranavalona I is pitted as a hostile, ignorant ruler who drew Madagascar back into savagery because of her policies. However, Chernock (2013) points out that much of the disparaging of Ranavalona I stemmed from western ideals and values. In essence, disparaging Ranavalona I was the method of showing displeasure at the fact that she had absolute power despite being female. Western writers of the history of Madagascar such as Robert Drury and William Ellis pitted Victoria as a gentle, feminine monarch who cared about her people. They assigned her with feminine qualities and deemed those as appropriate for a female monarch. However, they painted Ranavalona I as a regressive savage who did not care about her people at all, and who was anti-feminine. Her qualities as a strong leader made her an unfit ruler in the western value system (Chernock, 2013). Views of the west on the role of women would soon come to have an effect on Madagascar, and the access women had to power in that country.

Madagascar was ruled by women during most of the nineteenth century. The female monarchs who succeeded Ranavalona I included Queen Rasoherina who ruled from 1863 to 1868; Queen Ranavalona II who ruled from 1868 to 1883, and the final monarch before the onset of the French colonization, Queen Ranavalona III who ruled from 1883 to 1897 (Kent, 1962; Ellis, 2003). Little information was found during the research for this study on these latest queens, but it is worth noting that much of the history of the kingdom period of Madagascar that was explored tended to focus on the kings of the period more than the queens. Ranavalona I, however, is an example of the fact that the queens were not just figureheads, but held actual power. Her prominence in the literature may have to do with the fact that she ruled concurrently with Queen Victoria of Great Britain at a time when Madagascar was of strategic importance to the European nations. Even now in studying women and leadership, the content displays an obvious bias towards focusing solely on the contribution of men, but Malagasy women's historical access to leadership roles in their country cannot be denied. The unwritten constitution of the Hova tribe made no discrimination on the basis of sex for access to any leadership positions (Chernock, 2013).

Women were respected rulers during the Kingdom of the Merina. During the 63 years under French colonial rule in Madagascar, western ideas changed the country's culture and customs to an extent. Western educational and religious customs came to play a part in women's access to leadership. One of the reasons women lack access to leadership is because they also lack access to education. It was the western custom at the time for the French to only send their boys to be educated, and this system became imposed in their colonies, including Madagascar. By denying women access to education, the values that the French imposed in the country also denied them access to leadership. However, the Malagasy historical legacy of women in leadership is still present, so the idea of women in leadership positions is not one that is far-fetched or a foreign concept to the Malagasy people. This fact makes it easier and less unthinkable for women to attain leadership positions. Outside the concept of the country's historical legacy, another factor emerged from within Madagascar to explain the access that women have to leadership positions – that is their direct and active involvement in the political and social arenas of Malagasy life.

Activism

The French colonized Madagascar by 1896. During the colonial period, there was resistance to the French rule and a push for independence. In fact, there was resistance to European influence even before the colonization of the island by France. As stated previously, King Radama I welcomed European influence and sought to change Malagasy culture to fit western views of society. His changes, however, were not immediately met with acceptance. According to Rich (2004), when Radama I began to make these changes, which included a change from the traditional Malagasy haircut for the king, in 1822 five thousand Malagasy women who were of the aristocratic class gathered in protest to demand a return to tradition. Radama I, now influenced by European views of women, executed the leaders of the protest and demanded that the others return home to see to their domestic duties. The protesters did comply with the king. However, this event is evidence that even when Madagascar was a kingdom not yet wholly influenced by Europe, activism was utilized by women as a method of influencing the governance of their country. This legacy would continue after colonization and independence.

One woman who was active during the period when Madagascar was a French colony was Gisele Rabesahala. Rabesahala was on the leaders of the AKFM–Congrès de l'Indépendance de Madagascar during the French colonial period (Kent 1962). Kent argues that Rabesahala and her cohorts were radical in outlook, and as leaders of the AKFM, the party also became radical in its outlook. She became secretary-general of the party in 1959 and controlled its direction despite the existence of a president of the party (Thompson & Adloff, 1965). Thompson and Adloff (1965) claim that Rabesahala created a cultural Madagascar. And indeed, her activism during the fight for dependence led to her appointment as Minister of Culture and Revolutionary Art of Madagascar from 1977 until 1991 (United Nations Educational, Scientific, and Cultural Organization, 2014).

Previous to this she was also the first woman elected as a representative for the Atananarivo City Council in 1958.

Gisele Rabesahala's example shows that activism does increase women's access to leadership. Her activism during the struggle for independence paved the way for Rabesahala's appointment into a political leadership position. Additionally, the example of Gisele Rabesahala shows the importance of history to women's current access to leadership. Rabesahala's image and story have been made into a comic strip which details her struggles and activism for Madagascar's independence, and also other achievements throughout her life (UNESCO, 2014). It serves to encourage young women and demonstrates the power that is attached to past female leaders and the ability that their having existed provides to other women to gain access to leadership. Although past queens were not found to be utilized in this same way, it is possible to assume that they could be used as examples, because the presence of women in leadership tends to serve as an inspiration to other women to become leaders (Perkins, Haslam, & Kulich, 2013).

The period between Giselle Rabesahala's activism and contemporary Madagascar generated very few female leaders in the government. However, female leaders could still be found in other areas of public life. For instance, Lila Hanitra Ratsifandrihamanana, during the period from 1986 to 1998 was a researcher and teacher at the Higher Teacher Training School's Center for Studies and Research in Natural Sciences; she was the head of the center from 1993 – 1997. She then became the Minister of Scientific Research in 1997. In 1998 to 2002, she was the Minister of Foreign Affairs in Madagascar. Ratsifandrihamanana was also appointed as the Malagasy ambassador to various states in Africa (United Nations, 2009). Lila Hanitra Ratsifandrihamanana's example demonstrates that leadership and active participation in other civil areas of life can lead to leadership in general and political leadership in particular.

In the present period, other women have demonstrated that their activism opens the way to leadership for women. In the realm of political activism, there exist women like Saraha Georget, who is the leader of the Green Party in Madagascar. Another party leader is Brigitte Rasamoelina who is the leader of the Women in Politics Political Party (AMP). Rasamoelina was president of the Association of Women Mayors before becoming the leader of her own party which she reports currently has over 5000 members. Another party leader is Yvette Sylla, who does not call her organization a political party, but a development association known as Mother Madagascar (Women's Movement in Politics, 2015).

All three of these women are examples of political activists who have in a sense created access to leadership positions for themselves by virtue of their activism. Their interests in the political government of Madagascar, and their dissatisfaction with the political parties already existing led them to actively create and establish their own political parties in the country. Like Rabesahala, their activism opened their access to leadership. Bauer and Burnet (2013) note that in the case of Botswana, women are not very active either socially, politically, or with advocacy, and this has led to very low participation rates of women in politics in the country. Activism, therefore, plays an important role in women's access to leadership.

The 2013 Norwegian Embassy report on women in politics in Madagascar states that the current political instability in Madagascar is a deterrent to the participation of women in politics in the country, but that women's participation in activism is higher at this time because of the lack of political participation opportunity. Therefore, women are more active in seeking to influence their leaders through campaigns and other political activism. The formation of the Women's Movement in Politics (VMLF) group may be an example of this. The group aims to increase women's access to political leadership through various campaigns (Norad, 2013). One campaign includes the 30-50% movement, which attempted to increase women's presence in the Malagasy Parliament to 30-50%.

Another part of VMLF's activities is the creation of a handbook that contains information to educate the population on women in politics (Electoral Institute for Sustainable Democracy in Africa, 2012). While there is not one outstanding leader of this group, it can be argued that the group as an activist organization itself provides a springboard for women's access to leadership. For instance, one of the mainstays of the group is support for female candidates contending in elections in Madagascar; the group acts as a support base for these women, and as campaigners for them as well. At the same time, it also encourages its members to go to the polls and vote for these female candidates. Therefore, women's activism in groups opens access to leadership for other women whom they support in leadership positions.

Most recently, women in leadership positions have demonstrated their activism by advocating and encouraging women to vote. The first lady of Madagascar and the female ministers in the country organized a campaign to ensure that women knew they could vote, and encouraged them to do so (United Nations Human Rights, 2015). These women already in positions of power continue the tradition of women's activism by using their positions to empower other women.

Implications

What significance does this analysis hold? We hope that the findings here can lead to the adaptation of measures that can be taken in Madagascar to improve the access that women have to leadership. However, getting more women in leadership positions is not an end in and of itself; getting more women in leadership positions opens the way for more involvement of women in public life on a larger scale. When women are visibly involved, this prompts more women to become involved as well and to see that it is possible for them to participate actively in shaping the decisions of their country (Perkins et. al., 2013).

This research has also demonstrated that in developing policies to foment greater participation of women in public life in any country, research is a necessary step. The literature examined in this study tended to focus overwhelmingly on gender quotas as one of the main methods that may be used to establish greater equality in leadership (Krook, 2008; 2013; Bauer and Burnet, 2013; Ryan et al., 2010). Gender quotas are in fact the most popular measure currently utilized to increase women's participation in political leadership. In the case of Madagascar, gender quotas cannot be ruled out as a method to increase women's political leadership because currently, there are no formal or informal political gender quotas in the country (Southern African Development Community Gender Protocol, 2014). However, the effectiveness of gender quotas is questionable because there is a track record in Madagascar where laws and policies exist but enforcement does not (United Nations Human Rights, 2015). Madagascar's situation must be considered in isolation; measures taken by other countries to improve women's participation may not work in Madagascar.

The political context of a country is also important when attempting to increase women's participation in political and public life. There must be research carried out to determine what the political climate is in order to know what policies could be effective. Madagascar has been experiencing constant political upheaval, with the latest occurring in 2009 (International Crisis Group, 2014). This political upheaval has affected the adoption of measures to improve women's participation. For instance, there have been attempts to institute gender quotas in the Malagasy political system, but these have ended in failure in parliament (United Nations Human Rights, 2015).

This research attempts to serve as evidence that no one theory can universally explain women's access to leadership positions, and no one measure can be universally applied to increase women's participation. It is important to understand how women get positions of leadership both in the past and present. This can be done through research. The research also introduces the possibilities that historical legacy and women's activism may be important determinants of women's access to leadership in other countries besides Madagascar.

Women make up more than half of the world's population, yet as demonstrated at the beginning of this paper, this is not reflected in the gender composition of leadership of the world population. Additionally, this paper has pointed out that women's access to leadership may be increased based on their empowerment. The activism of the women in Madagascar mentioned here was a result of the women's empowerment of themselves as in the case of women forming their own political parties, and also through women's empowerment of each other, as in the case of the VMLF.

Concluding this part

Historical legacy does have an impact on women's access to leadership in Madagascar. While I was unable to prove any direct relation between the past female rulers of Madagascar and women's current access to political leadership, the colonial period example of Gisele Rabesahala did provide evidence of a female leader from the past being used to encourage young women in leadership in the present.

Secondly, the research showed that women's activism also had an impact on women's access to leadership. Activism led to women empowering themselves and women empowering each other, and this opened access to leadership positions. Women either formed their own political organizations or they ran for office with the support of other women. Either case would result in more women in leadership positions. Historical legacy and women's activism in Madagascar paves the way for women's access to leadership.

This research does have limitations. For instance, while historical legacy and women's activism have been proven to have an effect on women's access to leadership, the magnitude of that effect was not determined. The question of whether gender quotas may increase women's access to leadership more than activism, for example, is one that this research cannot answer. So while the possible implications for this research included the formulation of policy and programs to encourage women's engagement and empowerment, there is no guarantee that any policies or programs created will be more effective than establishing legal gender quotas.

Exactly how much historical legacy and activism matter in women's access to leadership, is a possible future direction of this research. Determining the weight of the other factors found in literature such as kinship ties, culture and the electoral system is an area that could be explored to be able to better determine the impact of activism and historical legacy. This further exploration could help policy makers better determine what programs should be put in place to increase women's access to and participation in leadership.

Madagascar Election

The Instant

Madagascar's presidential and legislative elections are scheduled for 2013 (possibly May). These elections could herald a fresh start for Madagascar which had been hindered by the intense rivalry between the country's two leading political protagonists: Andry Rajoelina, president of the incumbent transitional regime, and Marc Ravalomanana, the ousted head of state. Both men have finally indicated they will not run for office in the 2013 elections: keeping to their word is vital.

Regional and international partners are already coordinating their management of the crisis. They must now step up their efforts to steer Madagascar's political class and military towards the implementation of a settlement that maintains civil peace and delivers credible elections. Then, with renewed donor support, the country can hope to revive exports, investment and a sustained drive for poverty reduction.

Madagascar may not show levels of violence and traumatic disruption to compare with those in 'hot' crises elsewhere, but it is a slow-burning social and economic disaster. The overthrow of constitutional rule in 2009 provoked cuts to external aid and the exclusion of Malagasy exports from vital access privileges to the important US market.

Despite donor efforts to maintain a drip feed of support for critical services, the UN reports that deprivation has deepened, particularly among children, in a country where incomes were already among Africa's lowest. The crisis has also hurt a once vigorous manufacturing sector and threatens lasting damage to a natural environment of global importance.

Madagascar's economic development depends on full access to international aid, investment and confidence. If political manoeuvres or administrative failings undermine the democratic credibility of the elections, the international community and the African Union will need to refresh their strategy. They will need to reconcile the credible defence of democratic principles with reviving the development and growth denied to Madagascar's people over the past four years of political deadlock.

The Contextual

The current crisis in Madagascar has already lasted almost four years and is the worst since the arrival of democracy in the early 1990s.1 It is principally one of poor governance: an extended stand-off between elites and their close supporters over the fruits of power while the country treads water, the population watches helplessly and Madagascar's unique natural resources come under ever more pressure.

The dilemma for the international community international community has been how to help Madagascar regain democratic constitutionality, without legitimizing the 2009 coup – but also without penalizing the poor and weak by allowing the vacuum in governance to continue indefinitely.

The background is deep and complex. Madagascar has many potentially unifying qualities, shared throughout the 'Great Island', including a single Malagasy language, a general caution when it comes to foreigners, common cultural beliefs including respect for the ancestors, pragmatic respect for authority or le pouvoir (those holding office have usually had an advantage over the challenger), and an instinctive dislike for overt confrontation. However, it also has many ingredients for tension, dissatisfaction and – in the last analysis – some conflict.

Madagascar's pre-colonial and colonial history has left its mark on modern attitudes. The majority coastal people (known as côtiers who came from a mix of Polynesian, African and Arab descents) resented their 19th-century subjugation by the Merina plateau kingdom (of Polynesian descent), and this influenced the general trend after independence for coastal areas to gang up electorally to prevent a Merina presidency. Nevertheless in the last decade the tale has been different, with two Merina political leaders (Marc Ravalomanana and Andry Rajoelina) at each other's throats, indicating that other factors such as control of central resources, institutions and security may matter more. France's forcible control of Madagascar in the colonial period also laid the basis for further layers of difference – between Protestant and Catholic and between the Malagasy elite and the modern French business class, said to own 'over 80% of all medium and large scale firms'.2 Within the Malagasy political elite there has always been competition for control of natural resources. Modern discoveries of minerals and hydrocarbons have raised the stakes. And within the general population there have been differences between the urban population, with generally more access to industrial jobs, services and imports, and the isolated rural population.

These cleavages were suppressed to a degree under authoritarian colonial and post-colonial rule and to an extent papered over by a patronizing neo-colonialism. However, in the last 20 years they have been exposed under the rising forces of democracy and economic liberalism. As in mainland Africa, the fall of the Berlin wall led to democratization, signalled by the institution of a Third Republic in 1993 when Albert Zafy defeated the long-standing autocrat of the Cold War era, Didier Ratsiraka.

Madagascar's messy democratic 'merry-go-round'

Since 1993 there has been a messy democratic 'merry-go-round' in Madagascar, the main features of which have been:

- difficult and sometimes unconstitutional political transitions, often marked by disputed election results, confrontation and some violence;

- regular revision of the constitution and use of institutions and security forces by the winner to penalize political opponents retrospectively and consolidate power;

- leaders who have all blurred public and private interests for personal gain;

- the general personalization of politics, weakness of institutions and of democratic culture;

- some bursts of political/economic reform and engagement with the international community (under Prime Minister Norbert Lala Ratsirahonana in 1996–07 and

Ravolamanana's first term in 2002–06, followed by periods of stagnation; and

- the general decline of the middle class and of the quality of life and rule of law for the average Malagasy, despite some private-sector growth

Difficult democratic transitions: Ravalomanana vs Ratsiraka, 2001–02

The first shoots of democracy sprang up after the Cold War ended and the Ratsiraka regime fell – a period marked by violence following the killing of opposition demonstrators in 1991 by the president's guards and his loss of the subsequent election. His successor Zafy's ineffectual leadership squandered the democratic dividend he had been handed, although his time was made difficult by excessive political factionalism, with a plethora of political parties based around personalities and factional jealousies rather than policies. Ironically, Zafy was impeached by parliament in July 1996 under the constitution introduced by the new democratic movement to bring better checks and balances. There followed a brief reformist period of better governance under Prime Minister Ratsirahonana. However Ratsiraka was subsequently voted back into office in 1994. He unsurprisingly passed constitutional amendments to restore the overwhelming authority of the executive and return to the traditional subordination of parliament and the judiciary to presidential political influence.

The next major controversy came when Marc Ravalomanana, the mayor of Antananarivo, the capital city, who had used his milk/yoghurt commercial empire to gain country-wide recognition, won the first round in the 2001 presidential election but declined a run-off against Ratsiraka, saying he had won an outright majority and calling for review by the High Constitutional Court (HCC). The ensuing stand-off led to Ratsiraka's supporters blockading the capital, the mobilization of Ravalomanana's supporters and the spectacle of rival 'governments' and economic disruption, with Ratsiraka controlling the provinces from the coastal city of Toamasina. Ravalomanana rejected mediation attempts by the African Union (AU). Following a recount that found he had won over 51%, his presidency was confirmed by the HCC and took office, thereafter gaining the upper hand and international recognition. Ratsiraka went into exile in France.

Although Ravalomanana won parliamentary elections in 2002, he also resorted to political manipulation of the judicial system to intimidate past or potential opponents. Ratsiraka was prosecuted and sentenced to five years in prison in absentia. A former prime minister, Tantely Andrianarivo, was jailed and then finally allowed to travel abroad for health treatment. Ratsiraka's nephew, Roland, the popular mayor of Toamasina, was politically hobbled through a questionable persecution. Despite signs of discontent from the military, Ravalomanana won the 2006 presidential election convincingly. In subsequent parliamentary polls, questionable management of the voting process delivered an easy victory to his ideology-light Tiako y Madagasikara (I love Madagascar) political movement, whose cadres were largely drawn from executives of his TIKO business group (a movement thus vaguely reminiscent of Silvio Berlusconi's Forza Italia party model.)

However, supported by international financial institutions and donors, and espousing market-economy slogans, Ravalomanana had some success in his first term, advocating economic reform and development, and opening Madagascar to more foreign investment and global markets; foreign direct investment rose from $86 million in 2005 to $1.47 billion in 2008.

Yet, as time went on, he showed political naivety by failing to win over some key interest groups, including the Francophone Malagasy political old guard and some parts of the army. He became increasingly vulnerable when showing signs of favouring his own business empire and spending excessively (e.g. for a new presidential jet), blocking business rivals and intending to lease a large bloc of land to South Korea.

France was slow to accept that Ravalomanana should replace Ratsiraka. Its relations with Ravolamanana's government were initially cold. Although they improved over time out of pragmatism, they remained ambivalent. For his part Ravalomanana was perceived to retain a generally anti-French agenda.

There is a plethora of political parties in the country but four have dominated elections in the multi-party era: Association for Rebirth of Madagascar (AREMA-Ratsiraka), the National Union for Development and Democracy (UNDD-Zafy) and, more recently, I love Madagascar (TIM- Ravalomanana), and Young Malagasy Determined Party (TGV-Rajoelina). Small reform-inclined parties have often occupied the political centre between larger blocs, helping to form governing majority coalitions. Prominent regional politicians have also developed their own local political movements. As a rule, parties have tended to revolve around personalities and interests rather than policies.

Difficult political transitions: Ravalomanana vs Rajoelina, 2009

To some extent history repeated itself in 2009 when Ravalomanana closed down the television station owned by

Andry Rajoelina, the mayor of Antananarivo, which had broadcast an interview with Ratsiraka. Rajoelina was able to buy the support of some demonstrators and elements of the military, helped by Ravalomanana's grant of a pay rise to the police rather than to the army. Tension escalated, with more than 100 deaths and the harsh suppression of a demonstration outside the presidential palace. This led elements of the military to step in, forcing Ravalomanana to stand down. They then conferred the presidency on Rajaoelina. He described himself president of a *Haute Autorité de la Transition* (HAT) and pledged elections by October 2010. These have never been held. Instead, Rajaoelina held a unilateral constitutional referendum in 2010, the result of which enabled him to stand for election as president, since the age limit was lowered from 40 to 30 years, and to continue in power until elections at an unspecified date. Ravalomanana left for South Africa, where he remains to this day though insisting he will return. He has since been charged *in absentia* with murder and attempted murder for the killings of protesters outside his palace in 2009 and sentenced to forced labour for life. There is also an on-going legal case against Ravalomanana in the South African courts, instigated by Malagasy litigants and relating to alleged crimes against humanity for the same incident. This may have been a politically motivated attempt to prevent him from being free to campaign abroad against Rajoelina.

A Divided Society

The current crisis has deeply divided Madagascar's political class and has increasingly frustrated ordinary citizens. The latter have low expectations of politicians but the current hiatus, a virtual absence of government, has left most feeling particularly helpless.

Rajoelina and Ravalomanana seem to dislike each other personally. Their very different policy approaches have also contributed to the malaise in the body politic. Polarized visions have created divergent views, dividing many families, communities and churches – Ravalomanana is a prominent lay member of the Protestant church – as well as the business (local and international) community and donors. This should not be overstated, however, as the vast majority of the people probably feel excluded from the Antananarivo political game: they will rather be hoping for tangible improvements in their daily life, which require a return of normality, confidence, security and economic prospects. Moreover, both Rajoelina and Ravalomanana are from the Merina ethnic group from the central highlands.

Competing interests

Ravalomanana offered a vision that moved beyond French influence and 'neo-colonialism' to a globalized world, tapping into some neo-nationalist instincts, such as of those who resented the assumption that if children were not educated in French they lacked a proper education. In 2005 he brought Madagascar into the Southern African Development Community (SADC) and accessed $110 million from the US Millennium Challenge Corporation. He attracted significant World Bank finance ($38.6 million by 2007). His 'Madagascar Action Plan' of 2006 emphasized the rebuilding of roads, governance, education, rural and environmental reform, family planning, economic growth and use of the English language as a tool for engaging with global and southern African markets.

In contrast, Rajoelina offered youth, a partial return to the French and Catholic Church sphere of influence, and escape from Ravalomanana's domination of politics and the economy. Rajoelina scrapped plans for English to be taught in all primary schools and called for French to be the language of education.

Blurring of public and personal interests

As well as using the executive powers to undermine opponents (for instance, by closing down media outlets judged to be acting against government interests), both men blurred national and personal interests, although similar accusations could be made against previous leaders.

Ravalomanana gave his businesses preferential treatment across the board, including in the context of liberalization, which in some cases hurt the economic interests of opposition figures. His Tiko Group grew to become a principal government supplier and it was at times difficult to distinguish it from his TIM party since political advisers and many ministers were former Tiko directors. Tiko companies received many contracts, tax reductions and exemptions, although the largest winners of public contracts were the French Colas group and the Sino-Malagasy company SMATP.

The ability to grant patronage and contracts also benefited Rajoelina and his regime, one illustration being the increase in approved rosewood exporters from 13 to 23 in 2009. Statements have allegedly been made by Chinese traders (and denied by him) appearing to implicate Rajoelina in the illegal Malagasy rosewood trade. Illegal logging continues despite a 2010 decree prohibiting all exports of rosewood and other precious timber for two to five years; and it seems a ministerial order can allow such exports.

Churches as rivals not mediators

Churches play a large part in the life of the Malagasy. Whereas in previous crises the Malagasy Council of Christian Churches (FFKM), which incorporates the Protestant FJKM, Catholics, Anglicans and Lutherans, acted with moral authority as mediator between political groups, the FFKM and Christian followers in general were split in 2009. For some this meant an ethical vacuum. Not only were Ravalomanana and Rajoelina Protestant and Catholic respectively (the former being FJKM vice president), but Ravalomanana had created a legal partnership between his administration and churches, in the process raising perceptions of favouring the FJKM. Catholics kept their distance for various reasons, including the closure of a phone-in programme on Catholic radio, the expulsion of a priest and Ravalomanana's educational reforms. The fact that the Vatican was at one time one of only four states to present ambassadorial credentials to Rajoelina (France being one of the others) further undermined ecumenical unity and perceptions of neutrality.

The Protestant and Catholic leaders have since reconciled in theory, urging mutual forgiveness between their flocks. But various incidents, including the closure of a FJKM-supported station and arrests of some journalists in 2010 for allegedly threatening state security, indicate that the HAT may well continue to see denominations in political terms.

Economic development and business rivalries

While Ravalomanana opened the economy to the wider world of SADC, North America and Germany, eating into French commercial dominance, the current crisis has brought economic instability. Growth dropped from 7% in 2008 to 0.6% in 2009. Many foreign companies reviewed their engagement and levels of operation given the uncertainty of trying to operate in a legally insecure environment. Some foreign investors moved to a watching brief, putting new investment on hold, monitoring the political situation and suspending operations, Exxon (with an off-shore oil and gas interest) being a case in point. The United States, the EU, Japan, the World Bank and the African Development Bank withdrew support (except humanitarian aid), which had previously accounted for about 75% of government spending. The United Kingdom cancelled debt relief and British aid to Madagascar fell from £15 million in 2007 to £2.5 million in 2010. Some businesses closed as a result of the international sanctions.

However, the finance ministry and the central bank have managed to maintain basic fiscal and monetary stability. The national currency, the ariary, has mostly maintained its value. This has been achieved through tight monetary discipline at the central bank and through a strategy of austerity in public expenditure. Now reliant mostly on domestic fiscal revenue, the finance ministry has prioritized the payment of current obligations such as salaries, while cutting back dramatically on capital investment and development schemes.

The sharp decline in aid and preferential trade agreements, coupled with the drop in tourism and a global downturn in markets for Madagascar's main food exports (vanilla, cloves, coffee and shrimps) led to 228,000 job losses in 2010, according to the World Bank. In the Free Trade Zone half of the 350 export companies closed. The 2009 suspension of the agreement under the US African Growth and Opportunities Act (AGOA), which allowed the export of duty-free goods to the United States, caused textile factories to close or lay off workers. Madagascar had been one of the big successes of Washington's AGOA strategy, which was designed to encourage sub-Saharan African countries to build up a competitive manufacturing base. There were previously 50,000 people in AGOA-related employment (25% of the jobs in the formal economy) and a further 100,000 had benefited indirectly.

But exclusion from AGOA has pushed the development of manufacturing into reverse.

Regulation has weakened since the crisis and business has slowed generally. Exports have fallen (down by 50% between 2008 and 2010 according to the World Bank). Nevertheless the agricultural sector, although vulnerable to climatic conditions, has performed reasonably well; and fiscal and monetary policies have helped keep the macroeconomic framework under control.

Mining production has grown thanks to the development of two major new projects: Rio Tinto's ilmenite project at Taolagnaro in the far southeast is already in production, while Canadian group Sherritt (with Japanese and South Korean partners) is well advanced in the development of a new mine at Ambatovy, east of Antananarivo, which will become one of the world's major sources of nickel and cobalt. Local community concerns over the impact of Ambatovy have attracted little national public attention – a sign of how the normal processes of scrutiny, policy control and dialogue with international partners have been marginalized during the prolonged political crisis and the HAT's stand-off with donors.

The World Bank's Africa Competitiveness Report 2011 cites the top five constraints for doing business in Madagascar as government instability/coups, policy instability, corruption, access to finance, and crime and theft.

The instinct of some competitors marginalized by actions taken by Ravalomanana and his companies was to back Rajoelina even before 2009, and a number profited by his accession to power. For example it has been alleged that Edgard Razafindravahy, owner of L'Express newspaper, 'became an anchor for both Rajoelina's public and business interests.' Many in the business community now speak of an 'Anglo-Saxon'/French divide that developed under Ravalomanana and revealed itself more fully in the 2009 crisis, accompanied by street rumours that French business interests such as Total funded the coup, The sense of exclusion was also felt by those members of Ravalomanana's own party not closely associated with Tiko. Hence after the crisis TIM split into two factions opposing or favouring his return to contest elections.

One of the early acts of supporters of the new regime was to vandalize Tiko stores and any others deemed to be associated with the old regime. The threats, lootings and hijackings brought operations to a halt. At least 5,000 people reportedly lost their jobs and faced threats because of their association with Ravalomanana's business empire.

China's economic engagement with Madagascar has grown rapidly since 2000. Chinese investment was encouraged by Ravalomanana; for example, Sunpec secured offshore oilfield concessions and other construction and mining companies signed contracts. The HAT in turn has tried to compensate for the suspension of international aid by increased efforts, such as lifting Chinese customs dues for Malagasy exports, to encourage

Chinese and Asian companies. One such has been WISCO, which had shown interest but had not received a permit under Ravalomanana, for exploration of the large Soalala iron deposit; it was finally awarded the concession by the HAT regime, a deal for which it paid a $100 million signature bonus. Probably reflecting declining standards of governance and regulation, another company apparently now present in the country (probably reflecting declining standards of governance and regulation) is the

China International Fund, which has attracted international attention in Angola and Guinea for its opaque business practices.

The long-standing Indian-linked business community (karan) has also continued to pursue opportunities, sometimes in competition with China. The head of the Indian-owned industrial group SIPROMAD encouraged Saudi investment in the hotel sector, a commercial opportunity that had previously been rebuffed by the Ravalomanana government. Varun Madagascar, an offshoot of the Indian parent company and an early investor in agribusiness, has bought substantial tracts of land for rice, maize and lentil cultivation. The company assured the local population that it would not follow the Daewoo example and that land deals would be negotiated under fair contracts. However, prices reportedly negotiated with the HAT ($15 per hectare for 50-year contracts) seem significantly lower than in the Punjab. Another arm of the company made a significant rare-earths find, a business area of traditional interest to China.

Mining and extractive industries

Although not yet operational, in recent years a large number of companies have been negotiating and setting up hydrocarbon production sharing agreements and joint ventures. Madagascar has 20 oil/gas blocks onshore and 246 offshore. It was accepted as a candidate country for the Extractive Industries Transparency Initiative (EITI) in 2008 but the current crisis led to its suspension in 2011 'until the international situation was resolved'. Although the unity government Prime Minister Jean Omer Beriziky appointed under the SADC roadmap (see below), asked in 2012 for the suspension to be lifted, this was not agreed to, although it was noted that there had been 'impressive progress in EITI implementation'. A multi-stakeholder group has developed a 2013–14 work-plan for implementation.

Although mining production has grown, Rajoelina and his mining ministers have made various statements about large-scale extractives industries, along the lines that they wish to raise company taxes, to renegotiate the Mining Code of 2000, and to raise licence fees, port fees and customs dues. They have also spoken of possible nationalization or of the state taking significant stakes in companies. In some cases auditors have been sent to 'review' companies and NGOs, and there have been concerns that discrepancies arising from non-adherence to old rules or new interpretations of old rules may result in non-transparent 'rent-seeking'.

Some large companies, whose operations have a significant regional impact, had made large investments before 2009 and were either fully or nearly operational by time the crisis began. For example, Sherritt International, the Canadian-registered nickel/cobalt conglomerate, began operations in eastern Madagascar in 2012 – although remaining under government 'review' with the aim of converting to a life-of-mine operating permit after six months. Rio Tinto's Qit Madagascar Minerals ilmenite operation, which has 20% state equity, started mining ilmenite in southeastern Madagascar in 2009.

Growing poverty

While there had been some progress in economic and social indicators between 2002 and 2008 (despite continuing problems of governance, employment creation and environmental protection), poverty has increased significantly since the 2009 crisis, reaching 77% of households in 2010, the highest in Africa, with an estimated average income of $400 per capita. Madagascar ranks 143rd in the UNDP's Human

Development Index and is unlikely to achieve most of the Millennium Development Goals by 2015.

External factors are significant. The suspension of most official aid, which accounts for an estimated 40% of the budget and 75% of public investment, has brought a dramatic drop in access to education and health, and an increase in social tensions. Over 30,000 workers were laid off from textile and garments firms after AGOA access was removed in 2010, thus increasing tension in the informal sector. School entry levels have dropped and teachers have been on strike seeking salary increases. Donors have tried to soften the impact of aid sanctions by channelling some pay direct to teachers, bypassing normal government treasury channels. Growing differences in living standards between the urban rich and poor have also increased social tensions.

The 2009 crisis also brought a sudden drop in official revenue with a plunge in tourist figures. According to the National Tourism Office, the number of visitors declined by 56% in 2010. This had rebounded considerably by 2012, however, and some new community-run projects have also emerged.

In 2011 the UN Special Rapporteur on the Right to Food, Olivier de Schutter, called on donors and foreign governments to reconsider the sanctions because they were aggravating an already severe level of deprivation. He said levels of child malnutrition were now among the highest in the world, comparable with those in Afghanistan and Yemen; that the suspension of AGOA trade privileges had cost at least 50,000 jobs in Antananarivo; and that many female former textile plant employees had been forced to become sex workers to survive. De Schutter acknowledged that donors had sought to maintain large aid flows through non-governmental channels, but he added that this had not maintained sustained action to combat poverty. He also pointed out that if donors had remained supportive, Madagascar could have moved further towards self-sufficiency in rice (the basic staple), instead of importing 100,000–150,000 tonnes a year.

In July 2011 the World Bank decided that the damage caused by suspending all new aid to Madagascar was too great. It approved a new credit of $52 million for measures to protect biodiversity in the national parks system.

Environment under ever-greater pressure

Madagascar has perhaps 5% of the world's plant and animal species, of which 80% are endemic. Its unique environment has been under pressure for centuries but this has accelerated in the last 50 years as the population has grown rapidly and more forested areas have been made available for rice and other crops through 'slash and burn' agriculture. In 1990 Madagascar had 11 million hectares of forest and 11 million people; currently there are 9 million hectares of forest and 20 million people.

There seems to be a cycle to the illegal logging of rosewood. This may begin with legislation protecting forests that is not enforced owing to a lack of resources and/or political will. Loggers accumulate stocks while awaiting an opportune time for export. A cyclone, an election (requiring funds) or a political crisis may provide such an opportunity to lobby for an 'exceptional' export such as those that took place in 2000, 2004, 2005, 2007 and 2009.

Ravalomanana made some progress in his expressed vision to triple the amount of land with protected status and to protect endangered biodiversity. Nevertheless during his presidency forests were opened to exploitation. The sudden rise in the export of rosewood during the last weeks of his government in 2009 – under a decree authorizing export under 'exceptional' circumstances for 13 registered exporters – was a case in point.

The crisis, with the associated weaker governance and regulation and loss of security control, has increased the threat to endangered species. A range of reports detail the poaching of lemurs, rare tortoises, amphibians and chameleons. Thailand appears to be a major destination for their illegal export, with animal-traffickers keen to exploit Madagascar's political chaos and lack of law enforcement. In 2011 TRAFFIC, the wildlife trade monitoring network, reported that in a 15-day survey of 32 vendors in Bangkok and eight Thai provinces, it had found 591 specimens of Madagascar's reptiles and amphibians for sale. In one week more than 800 protected reptiles were seized by Thai authorities at Bangkok's airport.

Law and order

The HAT regime has had general support from the military. That support has probably been nurtured by granting many of their requests, including a range of promotions and a 30% pay rise (in stark contrast to the attitude to teachers and others). In June 2011 the army's chief of staff said it would 'take all measures necessary' to prevent Ravalomanana's return as it could threaten 'public order and security'. But not all officers supported Rajoelina, as shown by periodic unrest in the ranks.

The crisis has seen a general deterioration of law and order and security, linked partly to politics and partly to the declining governance, human rights and economic situation (with criminals perhaps feeling more licensed to break the law given the corruption or other questionable behaviour of those in power). Different parts of the security forces (military, gendarmerie, police) are factionalized. Some senior officers probably remain neutral but others seem to have varying political affiliations, whether national, regional or local. Given that military leaders have their own spheres of influence, security or support is sometimes 'contracted' in return for payments.

The crisis has seen judicial judgments that are influenced by the executive, as when the HCC laid down rulings favouring the handover to Rajoelina in 2009. New institutions have also been set up with the intent to undermine existing ones, including the judiciary and police; this has led to the release of some detainees condemned for human rights violations and an increase in politically linked detentions. A new Special Investigation Force was established partly to control demonstrations and to pursue high-profile targets.

Misuse of power and of state force has been a feature of many Malagasy governments, however. Since the return to democracy, military guards have been accused of killing protesters under different presidents. There have been mutinies of various scales, some successfully tipping the balance against the president (as in 2009), others violently put down (as in July 2012.)

In addition to an increase in petty crime, muggings and robberies, there has also been an upsurge in cattle-rustling and larger-scale violence by significant groups of bandits, possibly using arms obtained from the military on the black market. A particularly serious episode of cattle-rustling and gangsterism took place in 2012 in Amboasary, in southeastern Madagascar. It reportedly involved several hundred well-armed bandits, some of them apparently former convicts or soldiers, whose threat seems only to have been finally removed by citizens taking up arms themselves.

Rajoelina's search for legitimacy through *de facto* control

Despite international criticism and sanctions, Rajoelina has held on to power. And until a surprise January 2013 announcement that he would not contest this year's presidential poll he gave every sign of a determination to prolong his rule by securing victory in that election. Repeated diplomatic efforts were made to influence him and other politicians to restore constitutional rule through a roadmap to credible elections. Analysts following the various international efforts at diplomacy and mediation could certainly have been forgiven for mostly concluding that Rajoelina's ultimate objective was to legitimise his power – in the hope that this would lead to a restoration of international aid and support; his tactic for achieving this was to play for time – hoping that the international community would accept the *de facto* situation – while preventing his predecessor from returning to the country.

International Reactions

Madagascar merits international attention for three reasons:

- Its geo-strategic position, rich minerals, natural resources and commercial potential;

- Its unique environment and biodiversity, which is highly vulnerable to human pressure and climate change; and

- Its erratic performance in governance, human rights and tackling poverty.

The 2009 coup was a clear breach of constitutionality. A day after Rajoelina took power, the African Union's Peace and Security Council (PSC) invoked Article 30 of the Constitutive Act and the Lomé Convention and suspended Madagascar from participating in AU activities. The Southern African Development Community and Organisation Internationale de la Francophonie (OIF) also suspended Madagascar, while the UN, EU, United States and others condemned the coup and called for a settlement based on negotiations between the two parties.

Over the last years there has been a range of views expressed within the international community, particularly on whether, and if so how far and how fast, to compromise with Rajoelina and the de facto situation on the ground.

The UN position has been careful. In 2009, in the aftermath of the coup, Assistant Secretary-General for Political Affairs Haile Menkerios declared that 'The [Security] Council members expressed serious concern about the unconstitutional means of taking power by [Andry Rajoelina] and urged that there be a quick return to constitutional order through a transitional process that is based on consensus reached through wide participation of all stakeholders in Madagascar'. The UN's Credentials Committee avoided the issue of acceptance or rejection of Rajoelina's bona fides as president, but SADC member states initially voted against his appearance before the UN General Assembly. The signing of the SADC roadmap in September 2011 opened the way to his appearance.

South Africa's foreign policy opposes unconstitutional changes of government, which no doubt influenced its offer of temporary asylum to Ravalomanana and his subsequent invitation to President Jacob Zuma's inauguration. In turn this probably increased Rajoelina's suspicions of South African neutrality, at least initially. There have also been pressures within the ruling African National Congress to offer an African alternative to Western intervention in Africa's crises, in this case to French manoeuvring in Madagascar. France, with which South Africa worked closely to draw up the original SADC roadmap, nevertheless appeared willing to accept Zuma's leadership in taking it forward. In the roadmap, the return of the former president to Madagascar without threat of imprisonment has been a red line for the mediators.

The refusal of the EU, alongside African actors, to recognize Rajoelina and its readiness to reinforce this stance with sanctions as necessary probably influenced the position of France. The EU also anchored its relationship with Madagascar to Article 96 of the Cotonou Agreement, an instrument for enforcing essential governance elements of the agreement such as human rights, the rule of law and democracy.

France has traditionally had the largest foreign interests in Madagascar, with nearly 25,000 citizens and 700 companies in the country. There was allegedly close French involvement during the crisis when Rajoelina took power. Indeed France's first response to the coup seemed to be to work for early normalization, building on the de facto situation, by calling for quick elections. As time went on, however, there were signs of French disappointment with Rajoelina's broken promises and poor performance. France's ambivalent position was probably dictated by its national interest. On the one hand it was pragmatic, encouraging the international community to take account of realities on the ground and calling for the continuation of some development aid to address the declining socio-economic conditions. On the other hand France supported SADC efforts to exert pressure on the key political protagonists, in the hope of moving towards credible democratic elections.

France's position was also confused by the management of foreign policy under President Nicolas Sarkozy, in which political dealings with some African countries were largely entrusted to the president's own Africa team at the Elysée palace, marginalizing the foreign ministry (which was more closely aligned with mainstream EU policy). Some Sarkozy advisers were initially viewed as sympathetic to Rajoelina and hopeful this would revive close relations with Antananarivo. However, France moved gradually into the mainstream international community stance towards Rajoelina's continued non-constitutional rule. François Hollande, the Socialist president elected in 2012, has been determined to position France in support of African management of crises in Africa. His main focus has been the crisis in Mali, but his broad approach is likely to reinforce French commitment to the mainstream international community support for SADC's handling of the Madagascar issue.

Although the United Kingdom controversially closed its embassy in Antananarivo in 2005 as part of a cost-cutting exercise, the current government reopened it in November 2012. This can be seen partly as a signal of Britain's wish to use its influence on the ground in initiatives aimed at securing a democratic return to constitutional rule as envisaged by the SADC roadmap.

The OIF policy has not strayed far from that of France. The OIF called for prompt presidential and legislative elections as a solution to the political impasse. Indeed it offered material assistance to facilitate such polls together with the Indian Ocean Commission, to which France also belongs through its overseas department of Réunion. At one stage it also envisaged a rapid timetable although the UN considered that updating the electoral roll, the essential prerequisite for fair polls, would take a minimum of 10 months.

The US position uncompromisingly rejected Rajoelina's unconstitutional assumption of power and Washington still regards the HAT as illegitimate. Following the coup, it swiftly ratcheted up available diplomatic responses. Non-emergency aid was suspended in the immediate wake of the coup, in keeping with the position adopted by most European and African states. Perhaps the action with the greatest impact was Madagascar's suspension from AGOA trade privileges and the termination of the MCC programme. The United States has also supported the mediation efforts of the AU and SADC.

Chinese interests primarily rest on potential access to vital commodities, trade, cultural links and developmental concerns rather than geopolitical or strategic rationales. The community of 60,000 citizens is one of the oldest and largest in Africa. China's official line has reflected its usual policy of non-interference, but in practice accepting the international position that unconstitutional change of government must not stand while keeping channels open with the regime, including by maintaining technical and humanitarian assistance. In contrast to most other external actors Beijing has been less concerned to put pressure on the HAT than to preserve Chinese economic interests.

India's interests are also significant, both in geopolitical terms and through its well-established diaspora. There is an ethnic Indo-Pakistani community of between 15,000 and 30,000 in Madagascar. Since independence Indian entrepreneurs have penetrated the commercial sector to the extent that a report compiled for India's Ministry of External Affairs in 2000 claimed that business people from this community owned 50–60% of the economy – a figure at variance with estimates of French commercial dominance. There are allegations that some Indian business interests favoured Rajoelina during the crisis and have profited since 2009, including from lower regulatory standards. The opening in Madagascar of India's first overseas military listening post in 2007 signalled the country's geopolitical importance to India within the western Indian Ocean for countering piracy and terrorism in the Mozambique Channel, as well as for India's relations with Pakistan and China.

International and regional diplomacy

From 2009 to 2011 there were successive efforts by the UN, AU and SADC, sometimes supported by the OIF and IOC (which are part of the International Contact Group on Madagascar (ICG-M)) to mediate and find a roadmap, but these were sometimes hindered by imprecise mandates or dividing lines (e.g. between the AU and SADC). Although some progress was made by involving all former presidents (see below), most initiatives eventually foundered or came to little because they were seen by one side or the other as leaning too much against or towards Ravalomanana's right to return to contest elections. Over time there have been signs of 'mediation fatigue'. AU sanctions against key HAT individuals were introduced.

Initially, the reaction of SADC to Rajoelina's unconstitutional takeover was hardline, with talk even of military intervention. However, the organization gradually softened its stance to position itself as a mediator, acting with the support of the AU, the UN and the wider international community.

A central role in this focus on mediation was played by Mozambique. As a Lusophone country it may have been sensitive to the risk that a hardline stance by the mainly Anglophone and mainland SADC would simply fuel nationalistic resistance to outside pressures in Madagascar, a Francophone island with relatively slight cultural and economic ties to mainland southern Africa. (There was also a risk that SADC would be viewed by the Malagasy as hypocritical, given its lenient treatment of the hugely more repressive regime in mainland, Anglophone Zimbabwe.)

The former president of Mozambique, Joaquim Chissano, played the central initial role in the mediation, and this led to the first attempt at a settlement with the August 2009 Maputo Accord. Subsequently, much of the day-to-day mediation work has been entrusted to Leonardo Simão, a Mozambican appointed as SADC's mediator. But a key role has also been played by President Zuma of South Africa, who has sought to exert pressure in favour of dialogue and compromise. In late 2012, with Zuma preoccupied by domestic politics, President Jakaya Kikwete of Tanzania took over the mediation role. After Ravalomanana announced that he would not contest the 2013 presidential election, Kikwete received Rajoelina in December 2012 and sought to persuade him also to pull out.

Rajoelina then announced on 15 January 2013 that he would not stand in the country's upcoming election. Paradoxically, his transitional regime's hardline refusal to contemplate allowing the return of Ravalomanana as a free man appears to have broken the political logjam. Late last year Ravalomanana finally concluded that he would never be allowed to stand and campaign effectively, and therefore announced in December 2012 that he would not take part. This increased the pressure on Rajoelina, because international partners felt that the government had acted undemocratically by preventing Ravalomanana's participation.

If Rajoelina had insisted on standing, this would also have breached the AU's principle that power gained by force cannot be legitimately retained. There was a substantial risk that Rajoelina's probable victory would not have been accepted internationally and would leave the country crippled by continuing aid and economic sanctions. Rajoelina could still change his mind, however, and is continuing to seek ways to retain power. He wants to lead his party through the legislative elections as transitional president and hopes to win a parliamentary majority, which would give him continued political weight.

It remains to be seen who will emerge as credible candidates for this year's election. Rajoelina maybe positioning himself for a 'legitimate' bid to be elected president at subsequent elections.

A tortuous negotiation path

Under the auspices of the ICG-M, the Maputo Accord and the Addis Ababa Additional Act of November 2009, Rajoelina and the three former presidents set out an initial roadmap for returning the country to normalcy, comprising a Charter of Transition, a Charter of Values promoting non-violence, tolerance, reconciliation and mutual respect, and an agreement to annul criminal charges against the former presidents. Although the four protagonists agreed to an elaborate power-sharing the power-sharing formula, they failed to reach consensus on who would run the transitional Madagascar: government. Rajoelina then distanced himself from the power-sharing agreement, unilaterally declaring a government of national unity and setting his own timetable for elections.

In the subsequent efforts to move Madagascar out of its seemingly interminable political impasse, SADC became the key negotiator, with South Africa leading the way within a 'Troika'. In September 2011, after the earlier roadmap was rejected by Ravalomanana, Ratsiraka and Zafy, an amended roadmap negotiation by SADC was signed by the representatives of nearly all key Malagasy political leaders and seen as the path to normalization.

This new deal stipulated the unconditional return of and an amnesty for Ravalomanana and the formation of an interim cabinet in the run-up to elections. A new prime minister was appointed (Omer Beriziky, a former diplomat and academic) and a new 'national union' transitional government formed, although it ran into early trouble with opposition leaders who objected to the HAT's control of key portfolios. In August 2012 the council of ministers suspended the five members of the Ravalomanana camp who had yet to take up office. A parliament was appointed and the restructuring of the Independent Electoral Commission (CENI) – which had conducted the unilateral referendum called by Rajoelina – got under way, with its replacement by a new CENI of the Transition (CENIT), whose members were drawn from civil society, the administration and signatories of the roadmap.

SADC leaders met in Maputo in August 2012, following two inconclusive meetings between Rajoelina and Ravalomanana in the Seychelles in the presence of that country's President James Michel and President Zuma. They endorsed the calendar proposed by the UN and CENIT for holding a presidential election in May 2013; 'took note' of the proposal that 'for both leaders not to stand would offer the best route towards ensuring peaceful elections'; called for implementation of an amnesty for Ravalomanana; and, mindful of the potential for violence, asked the SADC Secretariat to send security experts to work out with Malagasy security chiefs the modalities for a secure environment for Ravalomanana's return.

The signing of the SADC roadmap roadmap led to more official contacts between the transitional government and the EU and its member states, including a meeting in Brussels between Beriziky and EU Development Commissioner Andris Piebalgs. The former announced that the EU had committed €17 million to support elections and the accreditation of some new ambassadors. EU aid programmes would also resume with the promise of €100 million in support of programmes of health and education, food security and civil society efforts to help the disadvantaged.

In September 2012 Rajoelina confirmed to the UN General Assembly that a presidential election would be held on 8 May 2013. However, his speech contained some language conveying apparent warnings to the international community. He asked for help to build a more promising future for Madagascar but 'without stifling' the country, and urged it to 'trust us and honour your commitments'. Rajoelina also emphasized the need for 'non-interference' and awareness of the 'reality on the ground'. He said the UN system 'cannot just be police'.

The UN Secretary-General has welcomed the roadmap and called 'for its full implementation in order to pave the way for peaceful and credible elections'. The UN has meanwhile contracted experts to assess the legal and technical framework for the elections.

Conclusions: The Way Forward

The SADC roadmap provides the basis for a transition to democratic elections in Madagascar, which if peaceful and credible could mark a return to constitutional rule. This approach has the support of the AU, the UN, the EU and key bilateral partners including France and the United States.

Presidential and legislative elections are scheduled for 2013 (with the presidential poll anticipated in May). Until recently implementation of the roadmap was hindered by the intense rivalry between the two leading political protagonists, Andry Rajoelina and Marc Ravalomanana.

For more than two years the confrontation between the two men prevented the country from moving forward to a new presidential election in which both could take part on a fair and open basis.

Having been convicted in absentia of corruption and human rights crimes in a politically motivated and questionable trial, Ravalomanana refused to sign up to a political settlement unless he was allowed to return to Madagascar and campaign for the presidency, unimpeded by the risk of arrest.

Rajoelina claims the question of Ravalomanana's return is up to SADC, but he has failed to overrule the HAT hardliners virulently opposed to the former president's presence on the island in the run up to the 2013 election. Although both men have now stood aside from the 2013 presidential polls, Ravalomanana's TIM party could be disadvantaged in the legislative contest by the enforced absence of its founder – especially if Rajoelina leads the TGV legislative election campaign. SADC and the wider international community therefore need to decide how they can apply pressure to ensure that the legislative contest is fair and allows all parties to campaign on the same basis.

There are three ways in which the international community might help reinforce the democratic fairness of the electoral process:

- Increasing international coherence and coordination between the UN, the AU, SADC, the EU, the United States, the IOC and the OIF;

- Supporting the SADC process, provided key principles are not compromised; and

- Effective and coordinated observation of the democratic process and elections, including an EU observation mission.

Against a background of deep division and distrust between Malagasy politicians, the international community should also consider an approach designed to bring about 'a new beginning' for constitutional democracy based on the following approaches:

- All politicians and media signing up to and abiding by a democratic code of conduct based on the highest African and international standards, including mutual respect, peaceful policy-based dialogue, accountability and transparency supported by civil society;

- Including all political parties in the democratic process – i.e. all led by their founding leaders if they wish, or with all founding leaders excluded from campaigning;

- Ensuring that Rajoelina and Ravalomanana keep their word that they will not be candidates in the presidential elections;

- The international community providing capacity-building and other support to ensure the independence of institutions such as the High Constitutional Court and the Independent National Electoral Commission for the Transition;

- A commitment by political and military leaders to protect human rights and fundamental freedoms; and

- Launching security-sector reform, including a commitment by the military to abide by the constitution and not to get involved in politics.

The withdrawal of Ravalomanana and Rajoelina from the presidential race has broken the fundamental political deadlock. However, optimism must be tempered by caution – and by a recognition that serious challenges still lie ahead. Awkward dilemmas remain.

Such an approach, if it led to real commitment by all Malagasy stake-holders, resulting in credible elections, would need to be sustained. Credible elections, if they transpired, might logically encourage the international community to build on such a 'new beginning' through constructive engagement, including by reviewing current aid and trade constraints. That in turn could bring positive benefits for Malagasy citizens through improved confidence, growth, social services and employment. Such an outcome of credible elections, if they transpired, would again emphasise the validity of the efforts of SADC, the AU and other international bodies in promoting democracy and better governance. And it would encourage increased Malagasy trade and investment with foreign partners who seek good standards of governance and rule of law, rather than the reverse, thus helping prospects for a virtuous cycle of growth and development.

Thus the international community needs to exert a strong diplomatic effort now. It should press for elections to be held on a genuinely fair and inclusive basis and to international standards, welcoming the agreement by Rajoelina and Ravolomanana not to stand but ensuring that all parties can engage freely in politics in the country. After four years, Madagascar has the chance of a fresh start. This is the moment for engagement, as these efforts could help Madagascar return to stability and prosperity.

Madagascar: Measuring the Impact of the Political Crisis

The Economy

Antananarivo, June 5, 2013_ Madagascar is a country with enormous potential. When it was not in crisis, Madagascar grew at an average 5 percent a year. But overall economic growth has been flat over the period 2009-13. Against a benchmark of 5 percent annual growth, GDP in 2013 would have been 20 percent above its current level. The gap between where the economy could have been and where it is suggests that the cumulative costs of the crisis now exceed US$8 billion.

Since January 2009, Madagascar has been in the throes of a political crisis, generated by an unconstitutional change of government, following the nomination of Andry Rajoelina who was, at that time, the mayor of Antananarivo, the capital city, as head of state. This was rejected by the international community. The political crisis and the enormous uncertainty it created for private investment acted as a brake on economic growth. Four and half years into the political crisis, the effects on Madagascar's economic and social outcomes have been very severe.

The lost years of socio-economic development

- The economy has stalled, income per capita has fallen: With high population growth (2.9 percent), the population of Madagascar has increased by over 3 million people from 2008 to 2013. As a result of economic stagnation, income per capita in 2013 has fallen back to its 2001 level.

- Poverty has sharply increased: Preliminary estimates suggest that, from 2008 to 2013, the proportion of the population living under the poverty line (which was already high before the crisis), may have increased by more than 10 percentage points. With more than 92 percent of the population living under $2 a day, Madagascar is now one of the poorest countries in the world.

- Social outcomes have worsened: despite crisis-related aid, the number of out-of-school children has increased, possibly by more than 600,000. Acute child malnutrition remains critical, having increased in some areas by more than 50 percent. Numerous health care centers have closed, and poor parents have had to shoulder a heavy proportion of the cost of putting their children to school, due to a lack of government funding. These developments put the welfare of future generations at risk. At this point, Madagascar will not reach most of the UN Millennium Development Goals (MDG) by 2015, even the ones which in 2007 were deemed potentially achievable (e.g., reducing child mortality, increasing enrollment in primary education, and eradicating extreme poverty).

- Public finances are increasingly under stress: Sustaining macroeconomic stability has come under increasing pressure. Tax revenues are falling, tax evasion has increased, and the capacity to hold the line on overall spending is strained in the face of political pressures, strikes, and shocks .While macroeconomic policy remains prudent, the risk of transferring the mounting costs of cleaning up a weakened fiscal position to the next government is real.

- Foreign aid remains muted: Aid dropped sharply in 2009, and has remained subdued. Official aid over 2009-13 dropped by about 30 percent, with a larger share shifted to humanitarian programs, raising issues of sustainability.

- Infrastructure has deteriorated: In addition to damages from cyclones, severe budget cuts in investment and maintenance have resulted in increasingly deteriorated roads, power and water infrastructure, impairing the medium- and long-term development of the Malagasy economy.

- The ability to deal with exogenous shocks is severely curtailed: Current risks to the global economy, especially in Europe, make Madagascar's economy even more vulnerable, given its dependency on exports and tourism. The country is also highly vulnerable to natural disasters (cyclones of 2008 and 2012).The political crisis is a major impediment to confronting and mitigating these shocks.

- The resilience of agriculture had helped avoid a food crisis so far, but new risks have emerged: The ongoing locust infestation threatens agricultural production and food security. The Food and Agriculture Organization (FAO) estimates that up to 60 percent of the rice crop is endangered. Here too, the political crisis acts as an impediment to mounting an appropriate response.

- Madagascar's longstanding governance problems have only been exacerbated: the weakening rule of law, increasing insecurity, poor governance in natural resource exploitation (rosewood, gold, precious stones), limited progress on the anti-corruption front, and the lack of transparency in the management of public resources have only become more pressing.

- The resilience of the private sector is increasingly being tested: There has been little new investment, domestic or foreign, in the highly uncertain environment of the past few years. The lack of overall economic momentum, the mounting infrastructure problems, especially in roads and electricity, and the deteriorating governance environment are hurting the short-term prospects of the private sector and its long-term plans. No significant number of jobs has been created, or can be created, in this environment.

Madagascar was already among the poorest countries in the world and the crisis has only made matters worse. The crisis is diverting attention from the crucial challenges the country needs to face and mortgaging the future of Malagasy citizens. From a strictly developmental point of view, a political resolution of the crisis is urgently needed. While the first round of presidential elections was scheduled for July 24, 2013, the elections have been postponed to August 24

www.ingramcontent.com/pod-product-compliance
Lightning Source LLC
Chambersburg PA
CBHW031110080526
44587CB00011B/904